DEFENSIVE TACTICS
with
FLASHLIGHTS

by

JOHN G. PETERS, JR.

Flashlight Instructor
is the registered
trademark of
John G. Peters, Jr.

Published by:
Reliapon Police Products
P.O. Box 14872 — Station G, N.E.
Albuquerque, N.M. 87111
(505) 296-1171

The author, the advisors and the publisher accept no liability whatsoever for any injuries to person or to property resulting from the application or the adoption of any of the procedures, tactics or considerations presented or implied in this book.

(505) 883-8803

DEDICATION

This book is dedicated with sincere appreciation to
Shihan "Tak" Kubota
the world's foremost police instructor.

ACKNOWLEDGEMENTS

The author would like to thank the following people for their assistance in the preparation of this work: George W. Slade, Professor Emeritus, University of Baltimore; Dr. A. J. Sullivan, Professor Emeritus, School of Public Communication, Boston University; Norman Bryden, formerly, School of Public Communication, Boston University; Donald Keller, Mag Instrument; Ralph Johnson, Mag Instrument; Sgt. Arnold Bernstein, Albuquerque (NM) Police Department; Officer Grady Tauty, Albuquerque (NM) Police Department; Special Agent James J. Trout, Jr., Federal Bureau of Investigation; David A. Slifka, Defensive Tactics Institute, Inc.; Michael Campbell, formerly, Defensive Tactics Institute, Inc.; Shihan Takayuki Kubota, International Karate Association; Harry L. Temple, U. S. Combat Judo Association; Dennis Anderson, Calibre Press, Inc.; Charles Remsberg, Calibre Press, Inc.; Dave Tracy, Calibre Press, Inc.; Massad Ayoob, Lethal Force Institute; Howard Berringer, Americans for Effective Law Enforcement; Vernon Turner, Claims Supervisor, City of Albuquerque; Ray Chapman, Chapman Academy; Joe Scuro, Esq., Nicholas and Barrera; Carol Charpentier, Code 4; Anthony Saggiomo, Pro-Lite; James Carley, Carley Lamps; Connie Mikolayczyk, Bright Star; M. Gary Patton, Los Angeles (CA) Police Department; David Maxwell, Washington Public Power Supply System; Denny Fallon, formerly, Police Product News; J. David Myers (he knows where he is); Special Agent John Desmedt, U. S. Secret Service; and James W. Lindell, Kansas City (MO) Police Department.

A special thanks goes to Bill St. George who is the artist whose artistic ability made this book clear and helped to advance the state-of-the-art in training texts. Also, Fred Woodcock who did the typesetting. A big thanks to Wendy who suffered through the typing of numerous drafts. Finally, thanks to the hundreds of police, court, correctional, and military people who have "street-tested" and who have definitely proven the safety and the effectiveness of the techniques contained in this book.

TABLE OF CONTENTS

FOREWORD

Finally there's a text on the defensive uses of the flashlight. The type of information which is presented in this book on law enforcement flashlight techniques has been needed for a long time. Until now, the flashlight has been issued and viewed by most law enforcement officers and administrators as an illumination device. Now, there is a definitive text showing us that the flashlight can be used for a lot more than just a light in the dark. Primarily, this text shows us that it can be used as an effective defensive impact tool.

Defensive is the key word when discussing the flashlight. Because many officers have used their flashlight as a baton, the flashlight often produces a negative image in the minds of administrators, of officers and of defense attorneys. The word defensive is often replaced with the word offensive.

Mention the word flashlight to some people and images of hitting people on the head, injuries and law suits come to mind. This text, I'm hopeful, will serve to erase these images.

I believe this text has three strengths which will help to create a new, positive image for the flashlight. The three strengths are: the techniques presented between these covers, the author and the illustrations.

The techniques have been proven to work on the street. They are also realistic and practical. These techniques are based upon the flashlight training program developed by the staff of the Defensive Tactics Institute, Inc. They have evolved and have been refined over the years, thus eliminating those techniques which weren't as effective as those which are presented here.

The author is another strength, and quite possibly the primary pillar of this text. Recently, I had the opportunity to observe John Peters during two separate 40-hour instructor-level courses. I was impressed by his vast knowledge of law enforcement defensive tactics, his professionalism and his understanding of real police problems in this area. It was the teaching ability of this true expert in the field which impressed me the most. John Peters motivates his students to work hard, and he has remarkable success imparting knowledge and abilities to them. Here he imparts his knowledge through words and illustrations.

The third strength is the presentation of the material. John chose simple and clear line drawings, rather than dull and cloudy photographs, to use in this text. I believe that these drawings will help to maximize your understanding and learning of the techniques. Also, the text is written in a very clear and concise manner. This, too, will aid you in the learning of this material.

In summary, I believe that this pioneering text will set the standard against which law enforcement academies will develop state-of-the-art defensive flashlight training programs. I'm also sure that this text will create the training standard by which agencies and officers will be held accountable by defense attorneys, by juries and by judges. No longer can the defenses of, "there's no training manual", or "there's no training program for the flashlight" be used by agencies or by officers.

Finally, I view this manual as a pioneering work which will help to legitimize the flashlight as a necessary and useful defensive impact tool. I also know that if the techniques contained in this text are properly learned, properly practiced and properly used, it should curtail the growth of the flashlight abuse cases which are cited in Chapter XIX.

Joe C. Mollo

San Francisco, CA

Joe C. Mollo has been a San Francisco police officer since 1966, and the Department's Physical Training Supervisor in charge of all defensive tactics training, since 1968. He has been studying the martial arts for over 26 years and holds a 5th degree black belt in Judo from the United States Judo Federation, a first degree black belt in Jujitsu and a brown belt in Karate. Joe received a Bachelor of Science degree from the University of San Francisco; he also holds California Teaching Credentials in Physical Education and Police Science. As a police trainer and martial arts instructor, he has worked with many experts in the field of law enforcement defensive tactics from the United States and from Japan.

INTRODUCTION

Flashlight.

To you the word flashlight probably means a portable, battery-operated, hand-held, lighting device used only when you are in a poorly-lighted area. And if you're like most of us, when you go to the drawer or to the tool chest and remove the flashlight you'll discover that it has dead or weakened batteries. The bulb, too, may be broken. For whatever reason, the flashlight either doesn't work, or doesn't work properly.

Unless you need the flashlight for an immediate emergency such as a power failure or to aid in the changing of a flat tire at night, you'll probably see no pressing need to correct the problem.

So far, the flashlight has been discussed as an illumination device. Now, let's change the focus. Let's think of the flashlight as a self-defense tool. It's an excellent idea, after all, there are no laws, to the best of my knowledge, which classify the flashlight, specifically, as a weapon. It's hoped that this text will prompt you and others to think of the flashlight as a defensive tool -- and not just as an illumination device.

Think about it. You can carry the flashlight while shopping, while jogging (color coordinate your flashlight and jogging clothes), while walking the family pet (especially at night), while visiting a bar or while traveling at night. And few people will question its presence; even fewer people will think of it as a self-defense tool.

This casual attitude toward the flashlight is not shared by you if you're one of the thousands who work in the criminal justice, military or security sectors. For example, if you are a patrol officer who is working a midnight shift, you must depend upon the flashlight as possibly your only source of light. It must work. It must be dependable because your life or that of another person may depend upon its functioning properly.

It may also become your first line of defense should a violator suddenly attack. Hence, you should have already thought of using your flashlight as a defensive impact tool.

Thinking of your flashlight as a defensive impact tool is not without its drawbacks. There is always the potential for abuse. For example, hitting a person on top of the head, unless it's a life or death situation, is hard to justify. Hence, in cases where this scenario has been played, the flashlight has come under microscopic examination.

A few criminal justice agencies, after reviewing alledged flashlight misuse, have banned the heavy-duty flashlight. And, yes, some have virtually banned the flashlight. Others, have issued the flashlight as the officer's primary defensive impact tool. Coupled with this decision was another equally important decision: to professionally train the agency's personnel in the defensive uses of the flashlight.

It is hopeful that this text will prompt administrators, officers and, yes, even you to view the flashlight as a legitimate and a necessary defensive impact tool. It is also hoped that this text will help to kindle the need for professional training in not only the flashlight, but also in other less-lethal and defensive disciplines.

Specifically, I hope that this text will help you and others to understand that:

- Flashlights do not hit people.
- Flashlights do not cause courts to award millions of dollars in alleged excessive use of force trials
- Flashlights do not set policy, rules and regulations.

These statements are true. Flashlights, basically inanimate objects, can not perform the above acts. People can, however, and sometimes they do commit the above acts. People, occasionally, hit other people with flashlights. Most of the time they're justified and operate within the use of force guidelines as established by the courts, and other tribunals. When these people fail to operate within acceptable parameters of the law, they most likely will go on trial where, on occasion, compensatory and punitive damages are awarded for alleged wrong doing. Finally, it's people who establish policy, rules and regulations governing the use of flashlights. The people who set these guidelines are often as ill informed about the flashlight as the people who the guidelines are to provide direction. Hence, one reason for this book.

One purpose of this book is to help legitimize the use of the flashlight. Of particular importance is the heavy-duty flashlight. During the past decade the heavy-duty flashlight has been given a bad name by many people. The focus has been on the flashlight or on the flashlight user. Seldom has the focus been where it's needed: training.

In the recruit academy you were, most likely, told that your flashlight was an illumination device. It was not intended to be used as a bludgeon. After all, that's why you were given a baton. And, if you were lucky enough to receive training in the proper, defensive uses of the baton, your fate was even more predetermined should you be caught using your flashlight as a defensive impact tool.

Granted, there are hundreds of incidents where officers have questionably used the flashlight to effect an arrest. And, if the department head is typical, (s)he either banned the heavy-duty flashlight or placed more restrictions on the personnel who are forced to rely upon it in darkness.

Policies, rules, regulations, memos and the like will not correct the problem. In my opinion, such actions only treat the "symptoms" not the "cause" of the perceived problem. The cause, in my opinion, is lack of legitimate and street-proven training.

All the memos in the world will not stop you from using your flashlight when the violator suddenly jumps you during a traffic stop or a domestic problem. Even though you're given a baton and a firearm, during a confrontation in the darkness, you will, most likely, have your flashlight in your hand. Hence, you're going to use it. Seldom, if ever, will you drop your flashlight to obtain your baton. The reasons: your light source is gone; and you don't have the time. Ideally, it would be nice, however, realistically you can't afford to do it. The stakes are too high. Your life or that of another is at stake.

Unfortunately, you, like most of your colleagues, are forced to undergo extensive firearms training, but are given little, if any, defensive tactics training. Rarely, are you given any realistic instruction on the **defensive** uses of the flashlight. Hence, you are better trained to kill someone with a firearm than you are to protect yourself with defensive tactics. Also, you know as well as the administration that shoot-outs are less frequent (most officers never see one) than are unarmed encounters. While firearms training is necessary, it should not be provided at the expense of other much needed defensive tactics training.

It is important, therefore, to design a contemporary defensive tactics system. This system should include defensive training in the following: unarmed self-defense; baton; handcuffs; flashlight; driving; officer survival; firearms; plus other impact tools and equipment.

Basically, the system must be designed with three components in mind: raw materials; supplies; tactics and techniques. The raw materials, in this case, are officers. The training program must be designed to meet "their needs" not the needs or the wants of the instructor.

The last decade has seen a change in the type of police officers who apply and are subsequently hired by criminal justice agencies. Few are the applicants who have prior military experience or who have been involved in rough 'n' tumble antics as they matured. More and more officers are college educated. Textbook theory initially replaces the experience of the street. While theory is good and has its place, theory seldom stopped a drunken violator from punching you out if (s)he is intent on doing it.

The training program must also be developed around the supplies (equipment) given to the officer. If, for example, officers are given plastic flashlights which will easily break, there is little point teaching them blocking techniques for the defense against a crowbar.

Finally, the training program must be rooted in good tactics and techniques. The tactics and techniques which are taught must be easily learned; be easily remembered; be realistic; and be street-proven. If they are not, officers won't remember them, and will not have confidence in them.

The contemporary defensive flashlight system of the Defensive Tactics Institute, Inc. (DTI) is based upon these and other issues. For example, the DTI-system is based upon the use of techniques rather than the use of brute strength. The results: female and small-framed male officers have both been able to easily and successfully use the techniques. In fact, many people have found that the DTI-system of training is a natural fit for both the smaller and the weaker officer.

In addition, the techniques can be applied from a "cold start". That is, you do not need to perform lengthy warm-up exercises before you can use or can apply these techniques. In my opinion, any technique which cannot be effectively applied without first warming-up is ineffective for the street and has no place in a defensive tactics system. And the techniques which are contained in the DTI-system dovetail, thus making it easy to go from one technique into another. This flexibility and versatility is important in combat.

As you know, a combative situation is constantly changing. The unknown thoughts and actions of your aggressor all too soon become intimate knowledge and reality. The defensive flashlight techniques which you study and learn, therefore, must also provide you with a chamelion-like quality; the flexibility to change, to modify or to integrate movement to match the demands and the changes of combat.

The defensive flashlight techniques which are presented between these covers possess these inherent qualities; however, you must first learn and then practice them. Practicing various combinations will give you the range of response necessary for combat. You should view these techniques as the ingredients from which you can make a good defense.

The techniques, and thus the system which is presented in this book, will eliminate the argument that defensive flashlight training doesn't exist. To the best of my knowledge, the DTI flashlight system is the first internationally-recognized system to be developed. Hence, the techniques which are shown and are taught in the DTI instructor and basic courses are based upon realistic, street-proven experiences.

In summary, I have tried to present the information in this book as simply and yet as comprehensively as possible. To help you learn the techniques, balance lines are included where necessary. This, I believe, gives a much needed "third dimension" to the drawings. However, the single most important factor affecting your safety is **professional training.**

Books and training manuals, regardless of their quality, can never replace actual training under the helpful eye of a professional instructor. When possible, enroll in a DTI flashlight instructor or flashlight basic course. The Institute's instructors are former police officers who have had street experience and who are dedicated and trained to give you the best training available in the field of defensive tactics. All of us subscribe to the philosophy that the classroom is the best place to learn, and the **only** safe place to make mistakes.

If you would like to be notified of our next training course in your area, please send your name, address and phone number to the Institute. The address: Defensive Tactics Institute, Inc., P.O. Box 14872, Station G - N.E., Albuquerque, New Mexico 87111.

I sincerely hope that you will never need to use the defensive techniques which are contained in this book. Should you be forced to use them, however, I know that you won't be disappointed in their effectiveness. Practice them. They work.

John G. Peters, Jr.
Albuquerque

ABOUT THE AUTHOR

John G. Peters, Jr., is president and founder of the Defensive Tactics Institute, Inc. He is also co-founder (with "Tak" Kubota) of the Kubotan® Institute, a division of the Defensive Tactics Institute, Inc.

A member of the United States Secret Service Defensive Tactics Advisory Panel, John has been involved in the study of martial arts and police tactics since 1965. He holds a third degree black belt in Jiu-Jitsu and a first degree black belt in Kodokan Judo. John is also a certified international Instructor-Trainer in the Kubotan® , in the sidehandle baton, in the straight baton, in the Immobilizer, in the Action Control Grip, in the riot baton, in handcuffing techniques and applications, in firearm retention and disarming and in defensive tactics. He is one of the world's leading authorities on impact weapons and defensive tactics.

Educationally, he was awarded an Associate in Applied Science degree and a Certificate in Corrections, both Cum Laude from the Northern Virginia Community College; a Bachelor of Science degree, Summa Cum Laude, from the University of Baltimore; a Master of Science degree from the School of Public Communication, Boston University; and a Master of Business Administration degree, With Honors, from the Graduate School of Business, Babson College. He has also done postgraduate work in governmental finance and accounting at Suffolk University.

John began his law enforcement career in 1969 when he was appointed to the FBI. While there, he received a Letter of Commendation for his Judo instruction from then FBI Director, J. Edgar Hoover.

In 1972, Peters joined the Northern York County (PA) Regional Police Department as a Police Officer/Self-Defense Specialist. Later, he transferred to the York County (PA) Sheriff's Department as a Deputy Sheriff. While there, Peters spent three years on the District Attorney's Fugitive Squad.

In 1978, Peters became the Staff Executive (civilian equivalent of Deputy Chief) of a Massachusetts police department, where he headed the Administrative Bureau (seven divisions) and the Planning and Research Unit.

Peters also served as Senior Research Associate for a Massachusetts-based criminal justice research firm. While there, he conducted extensive research into the area of the management of criminal investigations, and became one of the nation's leading authorities in this field.

An avid author, he has published over fifty articles, brochures, book chapters, handbooks and text books including: **Realistic Defensive Tactics; Official Kubotan® Techniques; and Defensive Tactics with Flashlights.**

John has also served as a management and a training consultant to many criminal justice, military and security agencies, including: the Los Angeles (CA) Police Department; the California Highway Patrol; the Las Vegas (NV) Metropolitan Police Department; the Seattle (WA) Police Department; the Salt Lake City (UT) Police Department; the San Francisco Police Department; the Escambia County (FL) Sheriff's Department; the Clark County (WA) Sheriff's Department; the North Carolina State Highway Patrol; the Massachusetts Criminal Justice Training Council; the Smith and Wesson Academy; the New Mexico Law Enforcement Academy; the United States Government; the Staff Training College, Montreal, Canada; agencies in Australia and in Europe; plus many, many more.

John is currently under contract with the Albuquerque (NM) Police Department as a management and training advisor. His responsibilities include the design, implementation and evaluation of a myriad of diversified and selected training programs.

Peters has also taught security management and other related security courses in the Security Program, Northern Essex (MA) Community College. He is currently a member of the college's Security Advisory Board. His biographical sketch is contained in **Who's Who in the East.** He has also served over three years on the Braintree Finance Committee.

DEFINITIONS

AMP hours

The current in amperes multiplied by the time in hours the current is drawn. Capacity is expressed in amp hours.

Appropriate Follow-up Procedures

Those techniques based upon departmental policy, rules and regulations or other legal guidelines which you select and use after effecting the arrest of an individual.

Average Life

From a given sample of lamps (bulbs), it is the average life of the total from the first failure in hours to the last failure in hours. An average taken.

Battery

Two or more cells connected together.

Beam Candle Power (BCP)

The amount of light energy measured in foot candles multiplied by the distance in feet squared from the source. BCP = Distance $(FT)^2$ x foot candles.

Candela

A relatively new industry wide accepted brightness term. The total amount of visible light energy emitted from a lamp as measured in an integrating sphere. m.s.c.p. (Means Spherical Candle Power).

Capacity

The ampere hours available from a cell or a battery.

Cell

An electrochemical system which converts chemical energy into electrical energy and also the reverse for rechargeable units.

Cell Reversal

The act of driving a cell into reverse polarity by excessive discharge.

Color Temperature

The visual radiation temperature of a lamp's incandescent tungsten filament measured in degrees Kelvin.

Design Lamp Life

Determined by the manufacturer under ideal laboratory conditions with **constant voltage applied** until burn out occurs. Rated in average hours.

Discharge

The conversion of chemical energy to electrical energy in a cell or battery.

Discharge Capacity

The ampere hours which may be obtained from a fully-charged cell or battery during discharge.

Flashlight

Generally, a small and portable electric light consisting of a minature light bulb and one or more dry cells which are contained in a cylindrical case. The flashlight is generally held in the hand.

Flashlight Basic Certification

The **official** certification issued by the Defensive Tactics Institute, Inc. to those persons who successfully complete the Institute's eight-hour basic flashlight training course.

Flashlight Instructor Certification

The **official** certification issued by the Defensive Tactics Institute, Inc. to those persons who successfully complete the Institute's twenty-four hour instructor training course. Once certified, the instructor may certify others in the Institute's Basic Course.

**Flashlight
Instructor-Trainer Course**

The **official** certification issued by the Defensive Tactics Institute, Inc. to those persons who successfully complete the Institute's forty-hour Instructor-Trainer course. Once certified, the Instructor-Trainer may certify others as flashlight instructors.

Flashlight Lamps

Commonly referred to as bulbs. The common types are low voltage, incandescent tungsten filament, gas filled and metal based. They are filled with a high pressure inert gas such as argon, krypton, xenon or halogen.

Foot Candles (FC)

The amount of energy from one (1) candle power source transmitted to a one (1) square foot area one (1) foot from the source.

Functional Life

The lamp life in hours as determined by the user. This takes into consideration the power applied, environmental conditions, mechanical stress, and when the minimum useful light is reached (end point). This may occur before "burnout".

Lumen

A term used more outside the U.S.A. 1 Lumen = MSCP x 4 or, 1 Lumen = 12.57 MSCP.

Out Gassing

The release of gas from a cell during operation.

Rated Capacity

The discharge capacity in ampere hours which the manufacturer specifies may be obtained from a cell or battery at a given discharge rate.

Self-Discharge

Conversion of the active materials in a cell from the charged to the discharged state on open circuit.

Secondary Cell

A reversible electrochemical system which may be discharged and recharged a number of times.

Service Life

See Functional Life.

Spillover

The radius of light from a flashlight which illuminates you during a tactical exercise.

Storage Cell

See Secondary Cell.

Strong Hand

As used in this book, your gun hand. That is, if you're right handed, then your right hand is your strong hand; the opposite if you are left handed.

Strong Leg (Foot)

As used in this book, your right leg or foot if you are right handed; the opposite if you are left handed.

Watt Hours

The capacity of a cell multiplied by its nominal voltage. The energy of a cell is expressed in watt hours.

Weak Hand

As used in this book, your non-gun hand. That is, if you draw and shoot your service weapon with your right hand, then your left hand is your weak hand.

Weak Leg (Foot)

As used in this book, the leg or foot on the opposite side of your strong side, as previously defined.

Chapter I

THE FLASHLIGHT AND THE 21st CENTURY

AUTHOR's NOTE: Many of the heavy-duty flashlights which will be discussed in this and other chapters are of a more complex design than the earlier and current plastic ones. While each manufacturer sets its own design standards, I have found the Mag-Lite to be extremely well-designed to meet today's demand for durability, for ruggedness and for survival tactics. Having worked with the Mag-Lite, I'm confident that it's not going to fail when needed the most. Mag-Lite flashlights have been used in the illustrations which follow. This does not infer that other flashlights mentioned will not work for you or withstand the rigors of training.

Although we have not officially entered the 21st century, we're close enough to use it in the chapter heading. One reason is that our actions in the latter part of this century, especially those regarding the use of flashlights, are sure to have an impact upon others in the future. Reflect, for a moment, upon the so-called constraints imposed upon us by the courts and by others from the past: Miranda, Terry, Mapp, plus many other laws and policies. Prior to discussing the future, however, let's take a look at the flashlight in the past and in the present.

THE PAST: AN HISTORICAL VIEW

No one really knows who invented the flashlight. History has indicated that Joshua L. Cowan, the inventer of the toy electric train, helped contribute to its development. Cowan lived in the latter 1890's, the same period in which the flashlight was patented. The American Electrical Novelty and Manufacturing Company held assigned flashlight patents, but no one person is credited as the inventor.

To some, Cowan should be designated the inventor. During the late 1890's he placed a dry cell (invented by George Leclanche in 1866) in a metal tube. At one end Cowan placed an incadescent lamp (invented by Thomas Edison in 1879); at the other end, a switch. In essence, he invented the flashlight. However, Cowan did not recognize the portable light's full potential. He used his light to illuminate flowers in flower pots.

In 1898, flashlights were first sold to the public, Most, however, were used as toys. The first electric exhibition which was held at Madison Square Garden in New York City, New York in 1898, sold flashlights to the general public. This was the first recorded sale of these lights to the public.

Flashlights, during this period, weighed more than six pounds (2.7kg) and contained a dry cell about six inches (15cm) long. Examples of these early flashlights are shown in Exhibit 1-1. These early flashlights would hardly recognize some of their "cousins" today. Major improvements have been made to the dry cells, to the lamps and to the barrel. The results: most of the modern flashlights are lighter and are more reliable than their ancestors.

THE PRESENT

Most of us were first introduced to the flashlight when we were children. We were probably given one as a present by our parents, and it probably didn't look that much different than the ones we see today in various hardware stores. While the ones today may lack the Lone Ranger, Tonto and Silver on the barrel, the flashlight still has the following basic characteristics: two or more dry cells; a barrel which is made of either metal or plastic and contains dry cells; a minature incandescent bulb at one end; a reflector; a lens; a switch; and a spring at one end to push the dry cells together making contact against the bulb.

The modern flashlight comes in almost as many shapes and sizes as people. It ranges from pen light size containing only one small dry cell, to the large two-foot long police-type flashlight which contains seven or more dry cells. Because of its reliability, its cost and its handiness, most everyone owns a flashlight. The flashlight is used around the world by hunters, by fishermen, by electricians, by motorists, by fire fighters, by police officers and by many others.

EXHIBIT I-I

**Showing Interior of
Case-with Battery
in Position.**

THE POLICE FLASHLIGHT: AN OVERVIEW

Since police work is a twenty-four hour business, the flashlight was a perfect fit for those officers who worked at night. Almost immediately after its development, the police adopted the flashlight. Originally intended to be used for illumination purposes, it quickly found many other uses.

One such use was as a weapon. Many times, both then and now, the flashlight became the substitute for the nightstick or the billie. And it wasn't long until two things happened: court cases developed, which examined the use of flashlights in "Brutality" incidents, and police administrators who were forced to look at the flashlight either as a substitute for the baton or as only an illumination device.

One of the first recorded court cases which examined the flashlight in a so-called brutality incident was **State v. Linville.** since this case is discussed in **Chapter XIX: Flashlights and the Law,** it will not be discussed at this time. Suffice it to say that it didn't take long for the issues of flashlights and excessive force to become married.....a marriage which appears to be lasting for a long time.

Administrators have also looked at the flashlight as a possible ersatz baton. While some of today's departments issue the heavy-duty flashlight in place of the baton, turn-of-the-century administrators didn't have this dilemma. One reason is that the early flashlights were probably used for illumination and for a baton. In those days, the use of force issue was not as microscopically examined as in contemporary times. Hence, the flashlight became a necessary companion of the officer. For many years a flashlight was just that -- a flashlight used for illumination purposes.

Many police officers found that the plastic flashlights would not endure the stress of daily police work. For example, if the flashlight were to be dropped or pinched in a cruiser door as the door was being closed, it would most likely break. Also, it was cumbersome to drop your flashlight and then remove your baton when involved in a scuffle. Most likely, the officer didn't have the time to drop the flashlight and then reach for his baton. (S)He had to react immediately. Hence, the plastic flashlight was not a good fighting tool. Either it got into the way, or if it were used, it broke leaving the officer with no light source and/or no "weapon."

Seeing this dilemma, the heavy-duty Kel-Lite was invented. The Kel-Lite was the brain child of Donald Keller who began to manufacture it in 1968. In an interview with Don, he told me that the Kel-Lite was designed as a defensive weapon, first, and as an illumination device, second. Finally there was a flashlight which was designed to be used in daily police work and in altercations.

Other manufacturers were quick to follow Don into this new market. In 1969-1970, the True-Grit heavy-duty flashlight appeared. Unlike the Kel-Lite, the True-Grit flashlight came apart in various sections. In 1973, the B-Lite, also designed by Don Keller, appeared on the market. One year later, the Pro-Lite Company began marketing the Pro-Lite. Yes, Keller designed the Pro-Lite aluminum model, too. The Pro-Lite was the first rechargeable flashlight. In 1976-1977, the Police Equipment Division of LA Screw Products, Inc., began marketing the Code Four flashlight. The year 1978 gave birth to the Streamlight rechargeable flashlight. Finally, in 1979, Mag-Lite made its appearance.

Many of these heavy-duty flashlights are of a more complex design than the earlier and current plastic ones. For example, Exhibit I-2 shows the design of the Mag-Lite D-size standard and large head flashlight. It also lists the nomenclature of the Mag-Lite heavy-duty flashlight.

The design of the original Kel-Lite and also many of those which followed, created a new era in law enforcement. The heavy-duty flashlight, by design, was now a defensive impact tool. It now entered the spectrum of defensive impact tools: the conventional baton; the sidehandle baton; plus many others.

Although it joined the impact tool "family" its users didn't get as educated in the flashlight's defensive capabilities as they did with the other members of the "family". Generally, business went on as usual. Little, if any, defensive training was given to officers in the uses of the flashlight. As a result, some officers began to use the flashlight as a baton, many times smashing people on top of the head. Both the legal literature and many police officers can verify this fact. It is no wonder, then, that this necessary and important police impact tool is considered by many to be in trouble.

When Don Keller invented the heavy-duty flashlight he did so to help the police, not to get them into trouble. He filled an existing gap. Unfortunately, most training academies, departments, administrators and officers didn't fill the "new" gap--mandatory training and certification in the uses of the flashlight as a legitimate defensive impact tool.

FLASHLIGHT NOMENCLATURE

Exhibit I-2

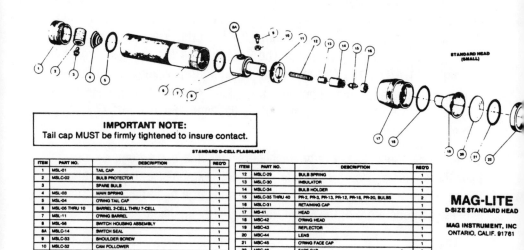

IMPORTANT NOTE:
Tail cap MUST be firmly tightened to insure contact.

STANDARD D-CELL FLASHLIGHT

ITEM	PART NO.	DESCRIPTION	REQ'D
1	MSL-01	TAIL CAP	1
2	MSLC-02	BULB PROTECTOR	1
3		SPARE BULB	1
4	MSL-03	MAIN SPRING	1
5	MSL-04	O'RING TAIL CAP	1
6	MSL-06 THRU 10	BARREL 2-CELL THRU 7-CELL	1
7	MSL-11	O'RING BARREL	1
8	MSL-56	SWITCH HOUSING ASSEMBLY	1
8A	MSLC-14	SWITCH SEAL	1
9	MSLC-33	SHOULDER SCREW	1
10	MSLC-32	CAM FOLLOWER	1
11	MSLC-26	RETAINING RING	1

ITEM	PART NO.	DESCRIPTION	REQ'D
12	MSLC-29	BULB SPRING	1
13	MSLC-30	INSULATOR	1
14	MSLC-34	BULB HOLDER	1
15	MSLC-35 THRU 40	PR-2, PR-3, PR-13, PR-12, PR-18, PR-20, BULBS	2
16	MSLC-31	RETAINING CAP	1
17	MS-41	HEAD	1
18	MSC-42	O'RING HEAD	1
19	MSC-43	REFLECTOR	1
20	MSC-44	LENS	1
21	MSC-45	O'RING FACE CAP	1
22	MSC-46	FACE CAP	1

STANDARD HEAD (SMALL)

MAG-LITE
D-SIZE STANDARD HEAD

MAG INSTRUMENT, INC
ONTARIO, CALIF. 91761

Although some departments made a serious attempt to train people with the flashlight, most did not. This has resulted in both intentional and unintentional misuse of this primary impact tool. The results: many administrators have taken the easy way out--banning heavy-duty flashlights.

Banning the heavy-duty flashlight hasn't solved the problem of excessive force, since now batons or worse yet firearms will be used instead of the flashlight. Time, I believe, will prove that the banning of the heavy-duty flashlight isn't the answer. Too much is at stake: namely officers' lives.

A partial answer to this dilemma is training. First, training officers in the **defensive** uses of the flashlight helps to insulate the administrator from vicarious liability. The officers were trained, hence there was no negligence on the administrator's part for failure to train. Second, through professional, legitimate and continuous training, officers have another alternative to the use of deadly force. Third, **defensive** flashlight training should reduce misuse of the flashlight. Finally, and not of lesser importance, such training may save officers' lives in the field.

Coupled with training is departmental policy and rules and regulations. These must be rewritten to accommodate the flashlight as an impact tool, in addition to its being an illumination device. A sample order reflecting these thoughts is presented in **Chapter XIX: Flashlights and the Law.**

Both training and policy will help everyone to survive, both on the street and in the courtroom. However, it takes a committment from both sides: the administration and the officer. Both must work in concert so the flashlight's image is enhanced in the community, in the department and in the courtroom.

The administration must recognize that there may be abuses even with proper training. Such a possibility is always present. However, to take an attitude that training officers in the **defensive** uses of the flashlight will give them a "green light" to kill someone is not facing the proper issue. After all, these same "would-to-be-killers" are issued a firearm.

Furthermore most agencies only train their officers to kill. Hours and hours are spent qualifying and requalifying on the range, with a firearm. Little time is spent, in most agencies, teaching officers less-lethal techniques such as the flashlight. Don't get me wrong, firearms training is necessary, but not at the expense of other defensive training. Fights are still more commonplace than shoot outs.

Officers, too, must pull their share of responsibility. Many will complain that the administration is training them only to cover its butt. To this I say, so what. Who cares what the rationale is as long as proper **defensive** training is provided. Once trained, then it's the officers' responsibility to police themselves (no pun intended) to minimize possible abuses. And not only abuses with the flashlight, but with batons, firearms and other impact tools. After all, you want to be able to carry these necessary **defensive** tools in the future.

THE FUTURE

Many people say that history repeats itself. To a lesser degree, the future uses of the flashlight by officers may reinforce what these people have observed. There is currently a small group of departments that have banned the heavy-duty flashlight and have issued the "old" plastic model. Should this become a trend, we'll have regressed to the use of turn-of-the-century equipment and tactics.

The primary reason given by administrators for the banning of the heavy-duty flashlight is to reduce the clubbing of people on the head with the flashlight. Now clubbing is really a Neanderthalic practice.

To help this regression from spreading like cancer, we must all work together to solidly legitimize the flashlight as an acceptable **defensive** impact tool. That's one of the goals of this book: to offer legitimate, street-proven and professional **defensive** flashlight techniques. Getting trained is the first step. Educating the administration so that it will change or reinforce its **defensive** flashlight policy is the second step.

Finally, if you need help, give the Defensive Tactics Institute, Inc. (DTI) a call. At this writing, the DTI has the only internationally-recognized flashlight instruction and certification program. The DTI has both instructor and basic certification courses. You could almost say that the staff of the DTI wrote the book on this subject. If you're as serious about getting trained as the DTI is about training, please write for more information. Only through professional, legitimate and realistic training can the flashlight survive the future as a legitimate, **defensive** impact tool.

* * * * * *

Chapter II

FLASHLIGHTS: Selecting the one that best fits your needs.

The thought process for selecting a flashlight is much like that for selecting a handgun. You should obtain the one that best fits your needs, and the one that best fits your hand size. Failure to include these two very important points in your decision making process may result in only one guarantee: your frustration.

For example, if you work as a plainclothes detective or as an emergency medical technician, you may desire a flashlight which can be easily concealed or be easy to handle in a closed setting, such as an ambulance. Hence, a two-or a three-cell flashlight might better fit your needs than a seven-cell flashlight. Conversely, if you need a high-intensity flashlight, a smaller two-cell would probably be out of the question.

So, how do you select a flashlight. While it's not really that difficult, there are some areas which you should consider. After considering these areas the chances of selecting a flashlight which properly meets your needs are much better.

To help you match the best flashlight to your needs, ask yourself the following questions. Following each question will be a short discussion of a couple of major points to consider in your decision.

The Flashlight Design

Does the flashlight reflect light? If the barrel of the flashlight, or any external part of it for that matter, reflects light you may wish to avoid it. For example, if you are a police officer who will carry the flashlight into search a building, you will need a color that won't reflect light. The reason: so a suspect who might be hiding in the building won't see your movement from ambient or artificial light which is reflected off your flashlight. For you, the most appropriate flashlight color would be a matte black. Conversely, if you're working in a medical center, the color of the flashlight might not make a difference. Hence, a blue or a red flashlight might be appropriate, especially if you're conscious about room decor.

Does the flashlight contain a spare bulb? A spare bulb may not be important to you until you're in a situation where you are depending heavily upon your flashlight, and the bulb suddenly "dies" on you. When the bulb expires, you would then probably give anything for a spare bulb. Many of the heavy-duty flashlights--some plastic ones, too--are designed so that a spare bulb can be carried in the tail cap.

Does the flashlight fit into your ring carrier? If you're a police officer or a medical professional who keeps a flashlight ring on your belt so that you can carry a flashlight with you, make sure that your future flashlight will fit properly. The design of some flashlight heads, barrels, and switches may prevent the flashlight from properly fitting into your ring. On the other hand, if you're buying a belt ring to hold your flashlight, take along your flashlight to make sure that it fits.

Does the flashlight have a lexan lens? The lens of the flashlight should be made of high-impact plastic. The reason: so that it is not easily broken. Lexan, a high-impact plastic, will meet this requirement.

Does the flashlight have any sharp edges? Sharp edges on a flashlight can cause unnecessary injuries to another person should you be forced to use a defensive flashlight technique. The cause of unnecessary and unintentional injuries is greatly reduced if the corners and the external parts of the flashlight do not have sharp edges.

Does the flashlight design make battery changing easy? This is extremely important, especially if you check or change your batteries on a daily basis. A poorly designed flashlight may cause you to waste time. Further, since little things tend to irritate, you'll become irritated on a frequent basis. Also, if you're in a dark location and need to change batteries, a poorly designed flashlight can cause you unnecessary problems. The best type of flashlights are those which can be loaded at either end. Some flashlights, by their design, require that you open both ends of the barrel to change or to load new batteries. This design is cumbersome when changing batteries. You may also forget to check or to load a battery in the front section of the barrel.

Does the flashlight design allow the light to be adjusted from spotlight to floodlight? If you're a police officer or a member of a search team, this feature can be of importance. For example, when searching a room or an area, opening the beam from spotlight to floodlight will give you wider scanning capability, Also, this flexibility can be important in police tactics where prior to searching a room you open the beam to flood (see Chapter XVI: Flashlights, Tactics and Survival). Although some manufacturers claim that you can adjust the beam on their flashlight, be cautious. To adjust some beams you must turn the head seemingly forever. Therefore, try out the flashlight **before** you purchase it.

Does the flashlight design allow for it to be mounted in your vehicle? For military, police, security, medical and truck driving personnel this point is vital. The ability to safely, to firmly and to properly mount a flashlight in your vehicle has many advantages. To mention a few: you know where it is when you need it; you know that it's not going to roll around the vehicle and get into your way while driving; and you can position the flashlight so that you can easily reach it and return it to its mounts.

Does the design of the flashlight switch assembly allow for the smooth rolling of the flashlight? This point can be ignored by the average person. The reason: (s)he, most likely, won't need to roll a flashlight across a floor or across the ground. For the police, the military and other law enforcement and medical personnel, however, the ability of the flashlight to smoothly roll across terrain my be vital.

For example, in Chapter XVI, **Flashlights, Tactics and Survival,** a rolling technique is shown for safely looking into a darkened room. If the flashlight cannot be rolled smoothly across the floor, the officer may subject him/herself to unnecessary danger: by walking into a room, or by having the flashlight roll until its switch assembly stops it, possibly angling it toward him/her, illuminating the officer, thus making him/her a target.

Does the style of flashlight come in various sizes? If the flashlight comes in various sizes, you must then only learn how to operate one flashlight. After learning how to operate one flashlight, your knowledge can then be transferred to another size flashlight. For example, if you learned the operation of a two-cell Mag-Lite, consistency in the design of Mag-Lites will allow you to pick up a five-cell Mag-Lite and use it without relearning its operation.

Is the flashlight part of a family of flashlights? It's nice to know that your flashlight is part of a "family" of flashlights. The reasons: for ease in operating only one type of flashlight; for uniformity in appearance; for repair purposes; and for building rapport with a specific dealer or manufacturer. When agencies or organizations consider purchasing a flashlight, the above points may become important.

Is the barrel of the flashlight made of heavy-duty metal such as aircraft aluminum? Aircraft aluminum is an excellent metal for the making of flashlights. It can be easily annodized, it is very durable and it's easy to machine. For you, it's important to have a flashlight that won't break should you drop it. Although a little more costly to initially purchase, it should be only a one-time expense.

Is the barrel of the flashlight made of high-impact plastic? High-impact plastic is much more durable than regular plastic. Hence, it can withstand more abuse. For many of the defensive techniques contained in this book, high impact plastic flashlights will work. However, most will break when doing defensive blocking techniques, survival techniques and may even break when dropped upon a hard surface. Most people who purchase the high-impact plastic flashlights find themselves having to replace them more frequently than the heavy-duty aluminum flashlight.

Is the barrel of the flashlight made of plastic? Inexpensive, lightweight plastic flashlights may be fine for using around the kitchen, but that's about all. Lightweight plastic flashlights tend to break easily and can be more costly in purchasing replacements, than in paying a little more for a heavy-duty flashlight. A few police agencies issue plastic flashlights to avoid injuring a violator should (s)he be struck on top of the head with the flashlight. Unfortunately, the plastic flashlight will seldom prevent injury. A plastic flashlight, when it breaks, will generally lacerate a person's skin. Hence, the violator may now have scars to remind him/her of the confrontation. Also, plastic flashlights may melt or become soft if exposed to intense heat, such as at the scene of a fire. Remember, if the flashlight doesn't look dependable when you buy it, it probably isn't. You'll pay the price one way or another.

Is the barrel of the flashlight smooth? If gripping the flashlight isn't important, then a smooth flashlight barrel is fine. However, if the ability to hold on to the flashlight is of importance (e.g., police work), then a smooth barrel will, most likely, not fit your needs.

Is the barrel of the flashlight knurled for better gripping? A knurled grip will offer you a non-slip gripping surface. Such a surface may be necessary for your type of flashlight use (e.g., police work, military, fire, security functions). The knurled barrel should also aid you in the performance of many of the defensive techniques which are presented in later chapters.

Is the tail cap flat on the end? A flat tail cap, versus one that is rounded or is bullet-shaped, is generally more effective when using defensive escape techniques with a flashlight. The reasons: the focus of the tail cap is better; the pain-compliance technique is more easily applied and is generally more effective; the flat tail cap won't puncture or cut a person's skin as easily as a bullet-shaped tail cap might; and, you can usually obtain a better grip on the tail cap-end of the barrel with a flat tail cap.

Is the flashlight waterproof? A waterproof flashlight is important if you work among sprinkling systems, in rainy areas or where the humidity is high. Getting your flashlight wet may cause it not to work. Rust, too, is a problem. A heavy-duty flashlight with "O" rings which seal various parts, may be your best choice.

Is the flashlight explosion proof? If you work in areas which contain gaseous vapors (e.g., you're a fireman entering a house filled with gas) you will probably need a flashlight which when turned on, won't spark, such as a Mag-Lite. Most of the flashlights on the market today have a spark potential.

Is the flashlight easy to operate? Take your child along to the dealer when buying your flashlight. If you don't have children, take along a neighbor's child. Give him/her the flashlight and see if (s)he can operate it. If (s)he can, then it's a pretty safe bet that anyone in your family can use it.

If you work in a hazardous profession (e.g., police, fire, security, military) ease of operation is important. For example, if you're in the dark and searching for someone, a complicated flashlight may cost you your life. Therefore, buy one that's simple to operate.

Is the flashlight rechargeable? There are a few rechargeable flashlights on the market. If you need the ability of having a "ready" light at your fingertips, investigate the rechargeable flashlight. Later, the rechargeable flashlight will be discussed in more detail.

Is the flashlight easy to carry? If your flashlight isn't easy to carry, it may pose more problems for you than it's worth. For example, if you need to only carry a two-cell flashlight, a C-cell size barrel may fit into your trouser or jacket pocket better than a D-cell size barrel. Further, if you are a police officer, the carring of a baton/flashlight might not only be hard to use, but it may be easily taken away from you by an opponent. Therefore, use a flashlight that is easy to carry and that meets your needs.

Can the flashlight head be removed? If the flashlight head cannot be removed, repairs to the flashlight might be hindered. Also, the changing of the bulb or the reflector may become more difficult. Finally, the removal of the head will allow you the flexibility to use your flashlight for various emergency tactics such as the rescue bar (see Chapter XVI).

Conversely, some flashlight models require that you remove the head to insert batteries. The Code Four is a good example. Some people would prefer not to remove the head and tail cap to change or to insert batteries. The potential to forget the batteries in the head portion of the barrel could prove harmful to you, especially if you needed a light source. If the head of the flashlight can be removed, make sure that it has been properly and securely tightened so that the flashlight will work.

Can the flashlight tail cap be removed? Although the tail cap generally is preferred by people for ease in the insertion of batteries, many tail caps for plastic model flashlights cannot be removed. The removal of the tail cap has many positive advantages: you can easily change or insert batteries into the barrel; you can use survival tactics as discussed in Chapter XVI; and various manufacturers house a spare bulb in the tail cap. If your tail cap is removable, make sure that it is properly and securely tightened so that the flashlight will work.

Can the flashlight be easily concealed? If you're a detective, concealing the flashlight might be important. For example, you may wish to carry a dependable flashlight with you on a daily basis. A four-cell flashlight will, most-likely, be too long to conceal; hence, carry a two or three-cell flashlight.

Concealing it on your body or in clothing may not be the only areas to consider. Possibly, you want to conceal it under the seat of your vehicle. If so, select the flashlight length and diameter which will best fit your needs.

Will the flashlight break or crack if dropped on a hard surface? Here, the entire flashlight is being evaluated, not just the barrel. If the chances of dropping your flashlight or of knocking it against objects is great (you're a carpenter, plumber or police officer), carry a heavy-duty metallic flashlight.

Will the flashlight float if dropped into the water? If you work on a boat, or a ship, on a sea rescue team or around the water, a waterproof flashlight will probably be a valuable asset to you. The reason: should you accidentally drop it into the water, it will float to the top, making retrieval a good possibility.

How much does the flashlight weigh? The weight of your flashlight may not appear to be important to you until you must carry or use it on a frequent basis. Carrying a heavy flashlight on an already overburdened belt full of other equipment may add perpetual misery to your work activities and to your health.

Weight may also have a direct impact on how easily you can use the flashlight. For example, if you have a small hand and you carry a D-cell, heavy-duty flashlight that you can't easily grip, you may be inviting trouble. First, another person may easily grab the flashlight from your hands. Also, the size and the weight of the flashlight may hinder your using it -- either as a defensive impact tool or as a flashlight. Therefore, make sure that you purchase a flashlight that fits your grip and isn't too heavy for you to use quickly and effectively.

To help you select a flashlight, Table 2-1 lists the weights (without batteries) of various flashlights. The Table also contains descriptive comments about each flashlight.

Since you probably won't carry the flashlight without batteries, you should add the battery weight to the weight of the empty flashlight. You can do this by simply using the following formula.

$$FW = FE + (BW \bullet N)$$

Where: FW = Total flashlight weight in ounces **with** batteries included.
FE = Flashlight weight in ounces **without** batteries included.
BW = The battery weight in ounces.
N = The number of batteries needed to fill the flashlight.

TABLE 2-1
Flashlight Weight without Batteries
(in ounces)

No. Cells Manufacturers	2 Cell	3 Cell	4 Cell	5 Cell	6 Cell	7 Cell	Comments
Mag-Lite	15.0	18.0	20.0	22.5	25.0	27.0	D-cell
Mag-Lite	11.3	12.3	13.3	14.3	15.4	16.5	C-cell
Mag-Lite	--	--	--	17.0	--	--	D-Cell Mag charger System
B-Lite	12.0	16.0	18.0	20.0	22.0	24.0	D-cell
Code 4	15.0	17.0	20.0	22.0	24.0	27.0	D-cell
Streamlight	--	--	--	9.6	--	--	SL-15
Streamlight	--	--	--	14.4	--	--	SL-20
Streamlight	--	--	--	16.0	--	--	SL-35
Pro-Lite	12.7	15.2	17.4	19.8	22.2	24.6	D-cell Standard head
Pro-Lite	13.3	15.7	18.1	20.5	22.9	25.3	D-cell Large head
Pro-Lite	6.0	7.0	8.0	9.9	10.0	11.0	C-cell Standard head
Pro-Lite	12.0	13.0	14.0	15.0	16.0	16.75	C-cell Pro-Loc
Pro-Lite	14.0	17.0	19.0	21.0	25.0	29.0	D-cell Pro-Loc Standard
Pro-Lite	15.0	18.0	20.0	22.0	26.0	30.0	D-cell Pro-Loc Large head
Pro-Lite	7.9	8.7	9.8	10.0	--	--	D-cell ABS Standard head
Pro-Lite	--	11.4	12.6	13.5	--	--	D-cell ABS Large head
Pro-Lite	5.5	6.1	7.1	8.1	--	--	C-cell ABS Standard head
Pro-Lite	--	8.7	9.8	10.0	--	--	Smoke Lazer Standard head
Pro-Lite	--	11.4	12.6	13.5	--	--	Smoke Lazer Large head
Pro-Lite	3.8	--	--	--	--	--	Mini lite
Bright Star	--	--	--	11.2	--	--	Model 6900 Plastic
Bright Star	--	5.26	--	--	--	--	Model 1626 Plastic
Kel Lite*	--	--	--	--	--	--	D-cell
Kel Lite*	--	--	--	--	--	--	C-cell

*Information was not received from Kel Lite regarding its weights by the time this book went into publication.

Now don't panic. It's really quite simple to compute the total weight of the flashlight. Since you already know the weight of the flashlight, all you need to know is the battery weight and the number of batteries needed to fill the flashlight. The number of batteries needed is simple: A five-cell flashlight needs five batteries.

Battery weight, too, isn't so hard to locate. Although the weight of batteries vary, the average weight of a D size battery is three (3) ounces; the average weight of a C size battery is one and one-half (1.5) ounces. To find the total accurate weight of your flashlight you should weigh the brand of battery which you're using.

After you know the weight of the battery in ounces, here's how you use the above formula to determine the total weight of your flashlight.

EXAMPLE:

Flashlight brand = Mag-Lite 4-cell, D size.
Flashlight weight = 20 ounces.
Battery weight − 3 ounces.
Number of batteries = 4.

CALCULATION:

$$FW = FE + (BW \bullet N)$$
$$FW = 20 + (3 \bullet 4)$$
$$FW = 20 + (12)$$
$$FW = 32 \text{ ounces}$$

As you can see, the flashlight weighs 32 ounces with the batteries included. Hence, before you purchase a flashlight, hold it, use it, etc. with the batteries included.

The batteries may reinforce your decision to purchase the flashlight, or "persuade" you to select another model which better fits your hand, your strength and your needs.

The Flashlight On-Off Switch

Does the flashlight have a slide-button on-off switch? Historically, the slide-button on-off switch has not functioned as well as the push button switch. Problems have included the slide button loosening, the slide-button assembly loosening and/or the slide-button when moved would not make proper contact with the batteries, thus causing the bulb not to light. Rain, too, has been reported to enter slide-button switches, causing the bulb not to work. Also, because of its design, you may not be able to smoothly roll the flashlight across various terrain. Manufacturers of slide-button on-off switches have, to their credit, redesigned many of the switches in recent years. Hence, their durability and their reliability should have improved with the new designs.

Does the flashlight have a push-button on-off switch? The push-button on-off switch is generally flush with the barrel on the flashlight. This makes for more aesthetic beauty and for the effective use of rolling techniques (see Chapter XVI). The push-button switches became popular among flashlight users after the repeated problem of early slide-button switches. For maximum performance, the push-button switch should be self-cleaning so dirt and foreign particles don't build up, thus hindering its action.

Does the flashlight on-off switch let you blink the light? This point may, at first, seem trivial; however, it's very important. The ability to blink the light is invaluable. The reasons: you can send messages with it (Morse Code); you can use it in survival tactics (see Chapter XVI) and you can use it when shooting a handgun (see Chapter XV). If you're employed in a hazardous profession, you really can't afford to be without a switch which lets you blink the light.

Is the on-off switch easy to operate? If the on-off switch takes time to operate due to friction or due to a build-up of dirt, it may not be the right one for you. For example, you don't want to fiddle around with a switch when you're in the dark and need light (e.g., police officer in a dark building). Also, the switch should be easy to operate so a child could turn it on, should (s)he need to use a flashlight.

Is the on-off switch designed to withstand heavy usage? If it's not, the switch may fail you when you need it the most. Even if you don't use a flashlight that often, a switch that is designed for heave usage should last you a long time.

Is the on-off switch designed to keep out dirt and foreign particles? If it's not, the switch may not work should the flashlight be stored or dropped in dirt or debris. Most flashlights are kept in drawers filled with many other items, in vehicles or in other places where dirt gathers. Again, your lifetime flashlights generally have switches that are designed to keep out dirt and other foreign particles.

Is the on-off switch designed so that you can easily roll the flashlight across a smooth surface? To reiterate, if your job requires you to roll the flashlight or to use tactics where the rolling of a flashlight is important, the switch design is of vital importance. Most slide-button switches will prevent the flashlight from rolling a full 360^0.

To compensate for the slide-switch design which prevents rolling the flashlight, some manufacturers have enlarged the head of their flashlights. Now, the flashlight is unbalanced, appears bulky and is, for some people, awkward to carry and to use. Hence, if you need this rolling ability, use a flashlight which has a flush, push-button, on-off switch.

Will the on-off switch design hinder you in the using of flashlight defensive control and restraint techniques? Most slide-switch assemblies will get into the way when using these techniques. Because of their raised design, slide-button switches will catch on clothing or will prevent you from getting a firm grip on your opponent.

Push-button on-off switches, too, can create problems. For example, one flashlight manufacturer places the push-button at the flashlight's center of balance. While in theory this sounds nice, from a practical and tactical view point, this design hinders your effective and safe use of various defensive techniques. For example, most of the techniques which are shown in Chapter XV cannot be as effectively or as safely used with the push button located at the mid-point of the flashlight barrel. To correct this problem, use a flashlight that has a push-button which is located behind the head of the flashlight.

Another problem in the location of the push-button at the point of balance, is that there is no consistency in the button's location. From a practical viewpoint, you can easily become confused when you're forced to remember the various locations of the push-button. There isn't consistency from flashlight to flashlight, even within the same family of flashlights. Again, to correct this problem, use a family of flashlights which place the on-off switch at the same location.

The Flashlight Bulb

Does the flashlight use a standard bulb? If it doesn't, you might have a difficult time locating a replacement bulb. Also, if you must travel a great distance, to purchase a replacement bulb, or wait a long time before the replacement bulb arrives by mail, the inconvenience probably outweighs the possible savings of a bargain flashlight. Therefore, carry a flashlight that uses a standard bulb.

Does the flashlight use a high-intensity bulb? If it does, make sure that it won't decrease battery life. Generally, high-intensity bulbs can be used in flashlights which contain three, four, five or six cells. A high-intensity bulb will generally:provide up to three times the usable light of a standard bulb; provide up to four times the range of a standard bulb; and outlast the standard bulb four to one. Of course with all of these benefits, the cost of a high-intensity bulb is about fifteen times as great.

Can the bulb be easily purchased? As previously discussed, purchase a flashlight that uses easily obtainable bulbs.

Can the bulb be easily changed? If you must dismantle the entire flashlight in order to change a bulb reconsider purchasing it. Changing the bulb should not be difficult. For example, if you're working in an emergency situation or crisis, the time it takes to change a bulb may mean the difference between living and dying.

What is the candlepower of the bulb? The term candlepower refers to the luminous intensity of the bulb. Basically, the larger the candlepower rating, the more intense the light.

Is the candlepower of the flashlight bulb over 30,000? If the candlepower of the bulb is greater than 30,000 the bulb is considered a high intensity bulb. A high intensity bulb will increase the beam and the brightness of your bulb.

What is the service life of a bulb? The service, or functional, life of the bulb is the hours that you use the bulb. Service life takes into consideration the power applied, the environmental conditions; the mechanical stress and when the minimum useful light is reached (end point). The end point may be reached before "burnout".

What is the average life of the bulb? From a given sample of bulbs, it is the average life of the total from the first failure in hours to the last failure in hours. For example, five bulbs are taken and tested. The failure in hours of the bulbs are as follows:

Bulb one:	4.0 hours
Bulb two:	1.5 hours
Bulb three:	2.5 hours
Bulb four:	3.0 hours
Bulb five:	1.0 hours
Total:	12.0 hours

Twelve hours divided by five bulbs equal 2.4 average life hours.

Does the bulb produce a bright, white light? The brighter and the whiter the light which is produced by the flashlight bulb the more its potential to cause the eye to react to excessive light. This reaction can help you to "stun" a person or help you to gain a tactical advantage over the person **(see Chapter XVI Tactics, Flashlights Tactics and Survival).**

Prior to discussing how this process works, let's first examine the structure of the eye. To begin, the human eye is covered with a tough coat called the sclera. Recalling your high school biology, you know that the front of the sclera is transparent and is called the cornea. Between the cornea and the lens of the eye is a space which is filled with a liquid. This liquid is called the aqueous humor.

Since I've mentioned the lens, let's look at the muscles which are attached to the lens. The muscles which are attached to the lens change its shape and therefore its focal length. These muscles enable the eye to adjust for sharp vision of near or of distant objects.

Behind the lens is an interior chamber which is filled with a jelly-like substance. This substance is called vitreous humor. The vitreous humor along with the lens, the aqueous humor and the cornea make up the eye's optical system.

In addition to these parts, the retina, the optic nerve and other parts of the eye are important to the vision process. For example, the image which is formed on the retina is comprised of rays that cross in the rear of the lens.

The front side of the lens contains the iris. The iris changes the size of the pupil radically, sharpens the image and protects the eye from excessive light. The iris of the eye is analogous to the diaphragm of a camera. As you know, the diaphragm of a camera controls the amount of light passing through the lens.

To summarize at this point, many parts of the eye can be compared to various parts of a camera. Here are a few primary examples:

Human Eye	Camera
Pupil	Lens
Iris	Diaphragm
Eyelid	Shutter
Retina	Film

At the risk of becoming too technical, let me continue the camera analogy. Just as you open the diaphragm of the camera for more light, so too the iris of the eye opens for more light, especially to see better in the dark. Conversely, the iris will reduce in size if too much light is present. Hence, the need for a bright, white light.

For example, research has shown that at low illumination levels the pupil size is enlarged to its maximum size with a diameter of 8-9 millimeters. As previously stated, an increase in light level will decrease the size of the pupil. The size of the pupil and the sensation of light depends upon two items:

- the intensity of the light source (the flashlight)
- the direction of the light beam when it reaches the eye

The length of time that the eye is exposed to the light source is also important. The reasons: as the exposure time decreases, the light source intensity must increase; and as the exposure time increases the light source intensity may decrease to a minimum threshold.

For example, you may only have a split-second to flash the other person in the eye with your flashlight beam. Based upon the above facts, the brighter your light beam the better for temporarily "Blinding" the person. Exneis' sensitivity curve shows that the highest visual sensitivity is reached between 0.2 and 0.3 seconds of observation time. After this short period of time the sensitivity of the eye decreases. The reason: saturation.

It should be noted that removing the light source does not stop the visual sensation. The temporary "blindness" will fade gradually. Hence, the flashing of the light beam into a person's eye will produce a temporary "blinding" which will give you a few seconds to either take cover or to take control of the person.

Glare, too, can be used to temporarily blind the person. Basically, glare is the condition produced by brightness which is greater than the luminance to which the eyes can adapt. Glare will most often cause annoyance, discomfort or loss in visual performance and visibiltiy. The intensity of the glare depends upon many factors, including: the size of the light source; the position of the light source; the luminance of the light source; the number of sources; and, finally, the luminance to which the eyes are adapted.

In summary, the more intense your light source, the more probable that it will temporarily "blind" a person. Hence, the use of high-intensity bulbs in your flashlights should give you the maximum potential for the causing of temporary "blindness".

TABLE 2-2

PR BULB INFORMATION*

PR No.	Part No.	Application	Volts	Amps	Candlepower
PR-2	MSLC-35	2-cell	2.38	.50	.80
PR-3	MSLC-36	3-cell	3.57	.50	1.50
PR-13	MSLC-37	4-cell	4.75	.50	2.20
PR-12	MSLC-38	5-cell	5.95	.50	3.10
PR-18	MSLC-39	6-cell	7.2	.50	5.5
PR-20	MSLC-40	7-cell	8.63	.50	5.0

*Courtesy, Mag Instrument, Inc., Sacramento, CA.

TABLE 2-3

Krypton Star High Intensity Lamps[1]
KS Series for standard carbon-zinc batteries*

No. of Batteries (C or D)	Model No.	Volts	Amps	Watts	Spherical Candlepower
2	KS2	2.4	.8	1.9	1.8
3	KS3	3.6	.7	2.5	3.0
4	KS4	5.0	.7	3.5	5.0
5	KS5	6.0	.7	4.2	6.3
6	KS6	7.2	.7	5.0	7.5
7	KS7	8.6	.7	6.0	9.0

[1] According to the manufacturer, the use of alkaline batteries with a KS Series lamp will **increase** candlepower approximately 20%; however, lamp life will be **shortened** by approximately 40%.

Average Lamp Life: 25 hours

*Courtesy Centurion Products Line, Carley Lamps, Inc., Torrance, CA.

TABLE 2-4

KSA Series for Alkaline Batteries[1]

No. of Batteries (C or D)	Model No.	Volts	Amps	Watts	Spherical Candlepower
2	KSA-2	2.5	.8	2.0	1.9
3	KSA-3	3.7	.7	2.6	3.2
4	KSA-4	5.2	.7	3.6	5.2
5	KSA-5	6.3	.7	4.4	6.6
6	KSA-6	7.5	.7	5.2	7.8
7	KSA-7	9.0	.7	6.3	9.5

[1] According to the manufacturer, the use of carbon zinc batteries with a KSA Series lamp will **decrease** candlepower by approximately 15%; however, lamp life will be **increased** by about 60%.
Average Lamp Life: 25 hours

*Courtesy Centurion Products Line, Carley Lamps, Inc., Torrance, CA.

TABLE 2-5

KSR Series for Ni-Cad Rechargeable Batteries[1]

No. of Batteries (C or D)	Model No.	Volts	Amps[2]	Watts	Spherical Candlepower
3	KS3R1.2	3.7	1.2	4.4	5.3
3	KS3R1.5	3.7	1.5	5.6	6.6
3	KS3R1.7	3.7	1.7	6.3	7.5
4	KS4R1.2	5.0	1.2	6.0	8.4
4	KS4R1.5	5.0	1.5	7.5	10.0
4	KS4R1.7	5.0	1.7	8.5	12.0
5	KS5R1.2	6.0	1.2	7.2	11.0
5	KS5R1.5	6.0	1.5	9.0	13.7
5	KS5R1.7	6.0	1.7	10.2	15.3

[1] Regarding KSR Series Lamps, the use of carbon zinc or alkaline batteries will dramatically **reduce** battery life.

[2] According to the manufacturer, KSR Series lamps are available in three amperage ratings. Hence, the higher the amperage rating, the brighter the lamp, and the sooner your ni-cad batteries will need recharging.

CAUTION: The KSR Series lamps burn hot enough to damage some plastic reflectors.
Average Lamp Life: 25 hours

*Courtesy Centurion Products Line, Carley Lamps, Inc., Torrance, CA.

The Flashlight Battery

Does the flashlight use standard batteries? If it doesn't, you might have a difficult time locating replacement batteries...especially if you're out of town. Also, if you must travel a great distance to purchase replacement batteries or wait a long time before the replacement batteries arrive by mail, the inconvenience probably outweighs the possible savings of the flashlight's initial cost. Therefore, carry a flashlight that uses a standard bulb.

Does the flashlight use C-cell size batteries? If it does, purchase batteries that will give you the most life. The heavy-duty battery is an example of such a battery. Brand name C-cell batteries should give you the best performance. When you purchase batteries, determine how much you will use your flashlight. The reason: heavy-duty, metal clad or alkaline batteries are not recommended for your flashlight if it isn't going to be used on a frequent basis.

Does the flashlight use D-cell size batteries? If it does, purchase batteries that will give you the most life. The heavy-duty battery is an example of such a battery. Brand name D-cell batteries should give you the best performance. When you purchase batteries, determine how much you will use your flashlight. The reason: heavy-duty, metal clad or alkaline batteries are not recommended for your flashlight if it isn't going to be used on a frequent basis.

Does the flashlight use cartridge-type batteries? Cartridge-type batteries are as the name implies--a cartridge. Basically, they are a grouping of separate batteries encased in a vertical format to form a single unit. Looking like a shotgun cartridge, they are easy to "load" into the barrel of the flashlight. Apparent advantages of the cartridge-type battery packs are: a replacement of individual batteries; a reduction in take-home pilferage (they won't fit most toys, radios or trouser pockets); and a cartridge-type battery pack is easier to "load" under stressful conditions. They fit easily into most glove boxes, too.

Does the flashlight use rechargeable batteries? If it does, ask the dealer whether the flashlight uses a rechargeable battery pack or rechargeable batteries. Also, find out how long it takes to recharge the batteries. Finally, ask how long the "on-time" is per charge. For example, the "on-time" of the Mag-Charger System is 1¾ hours per charge.

Can the batteries be easily purchased? If you can't easily locate batteries, your flashlight may not function when you need it because you can't find the proper size batteries. Also, if you must travel a great distance to purchase new batteries or wait a long time before the new batteries arrive (as might be the case for cartridge batteries), the inconvenience probably outweighs the possible savings of a bargain flashlight. Therefore, carry a flashlight that uses standard, available batteries.

Can the batteries be easily inserted? If your son or daughter, who is six years old, has trouble inserting the batteries throw out the flashlight. The reason: it's probably too complicated for you to use, too. If you needed to change batteries in an emergency and you didn't have much time, hard-to-insert batteries might cost you or someone else their life.

As previously mentioned, one flashlight manufacturer requires you to remove both the head and the tail cap to insert batteries. The reason: the modular design of the flashlight, coupled with the switch at the flashlight's balance point, force the insertion of batteries at both ends. And, if you forget to place batteries in either end, and you attempt to use the flashlight during an emergency, its failure may cost lives or serious injuries to yourself or to others.

Can the batteries be easily removed? This is basically the flip-side of the previous discussion. Removing batteries in a timely manner so that you can easily replace them is vital in emergency situations for the above life-saving reasons.

What is the discharge capacity of the battery? The discharge capacity of a battery is the ampere hours which may be obtained from a fully-charged battery during discharge. To find out, ask the battery salesperson.

What is the rated capacity of the battery? The rated capacity is the discharge capacity in ampere hours which the manufacturer states can be obtained from a battery at a given discharge rate. Many battery packages show the rated capacity.

The Rechargeable Flashlight

Can you justify the purchase of a rechargeable flashlight? There are two basic reasons for purchasing an item; you either **want** it or you **need** it. The **wanting** of a rechargeable flashlight to simply "keep up with the Joneses" may help you to rationalize your purchasing decision. However, deciding upon whether or not you actually have a need for a rechargeable flashlight is another issue.

Now don't get me wrong, we all tend to purchase things that we want but actually don't need. If you want a rechargeable flashlight, then go buy one. Your want is your justification. However, since they cost about $100, a little more thought may be necessary to justify the purchase. Besides, you probably need to convince another person (like you wife) that you really **need** the rechargeable flashlight. Therefore, to fully convince yourself or another person of the need, you should be able to justify it professionally and/or economically.

In most cases you can more easily justify the need for this state-of-the-art flashlight from a professional viewpoint. For example, if you're a police officer there is no question that a rechargeable flashlight should out-perform any conventional flashlight. The very fact that it can be recharged while you are driving almost insures you a charged flashlight every time that you need it to check out open buildings, basements and other darkened areas. Clearly, no one could effectively argue against your proposed purchase for safety reasons. A flashlight with the capability of always having recharged batteries to provide you with excellent light in dark and dangerous situations is a tough issue to debate.

To justify the purchase from an economic viewpoint, you should take a similar position. Lead the debate using safety as the common denominator. Spending $100 today on a state-of-the-art flashlight may save your life since it shouldn't fail you when you most need it. Conversely, spending $10 on a "disposable" flashlight might indicate the value of your life-- disposable. Besides, if you need it for your employment, you can probably use it as a tax deduction.

Can the charger unit be used at home? Even if you have and use a vehicle charger unit, you'll probably desire to have one at home. The reasons: you will want the flashlight ready to use at home; you will not always leave it in your vehicle; and you will want to "guarantee" that the flashlight is always fully-charged. Again, for economical reasons, you should purchase a charger that can be used in both your home and your vehicle.

Can the charger unit be mounted in any position? Some charger units can only be mounted, and hence will only work where the the flashlight is inserted, head pointing upward. Other charger units, such as the Mag Charger, can be mounted in any position. These latter units can give you versatility, which your needs may demand.

Can the charger unit be installed easily, quickly and economically? Obviously, if the charger unit can be installed with ease, with little time and with little cost you'll benefit. If you must leave your vehicle at an installer's shop or if you must hire someone to install it, the inconvenience and the cost may become prohibitive.

Can your current flashlight be easily converted into a rechargeable one? There are tail caps available for certain models of standard heavy-duty metal flashlights which will convert them into rechargeable ones. I have not had any personal experiences with these conversion tail caps and therefore can only tell you to check them out for yourself.

Does the charger unit have a charging-indicator light to show you when it's on? If the charger unit does not, you might be in for a big surprise. For example, you may think that it's on and charging when it isn't, or it may be broken. Therefore, I recommend a charger unit with an "on" indicator light.

Does the rechargeable flashlight use a standard bulb? If it does, then use the proper bulb. A high-intensity bulb, such as the Mag-Num Star, should give you twice the usable light with up to three (3) times the life span of standard bulbs. For example, the Mag-Num Star, high-intensity Krypton bulb, has a peak candlepower of 30,000. Again, failure to use the proper bulb for the flashlight might result in its failure to work properly.

What type of batteries must be used in the flashlight? Rechargeable flashlights generally require special batteries. For example, the Mag-Charger System uses a specially-designed battery pack. Installing the wrong batteries could harm the flashlight. Hence, to guarantee best results, know the battery requirements before you insert them.

What is the "on-time" per charge? "On-time" simply means how long you can continuously use the flashlight without recharging it. For example, the Mag-Charger lists its on-time as one and three-quarter (1¾) hours. Obviously, the higher the on-time the longer you can stay away from your charger. This feature may be important if you are a police officer, a fire-fighter or a rescue worker. The reason: it might become impractical for you to use a rechargeable flashlight if the on-time was very small, say thirty (30) minutes. From a practical viewpoint, you couldn't do too much or go very far.

What is the "track record" of the charger system? This issue is too important to take lightly. After all, you're going to spend around $100 on the system. One system I've been told, allegedly burns-out the vehicle charger unit if the temperature gets too cold outside the vehicle. Obviously, this unit should be avoided. Therefore, shop around, ask a lot of questions and then select the system which has the best "track record".

The Accessories

Can accessories be added to the flashlight? This may become important to you, especially if you plan to use your flashlight in tactical situations (e.g., military or police operations). For example, can an "O" ring be placed on the head so that the flashlight can be rolled smoothly across a floor.

Can traffic wands be easily attached to the flashlight head? If you direct traffic at motor vehicle accidents, at fires, etc., the attaching of a traffic wand may be important to you. The reasons: safety and flexibility of your flashlight. Make sure that the traffic wand can be easily attached and removed from the head. The reasons: so that you don't waste time attaching it; so that you don't waste time removing it; and so that your traffic wand sticks or falls off when you don't want it to do so.

The Manufacturer

Is the flashlight made by a well-known and reputable manufacturer? If it's not, you might have trouble obtaining parts or repairs. Even a large manufacturer can go out of business, but the chances aren't as great as the smaller company. Select a reputable manufacturer and you'll most likely receive a reputable flashlight.

What guarantee or warranty does the manufacturer give its flashlight? Simply reading the guarantee or warranty card will tell you how long the manufacturer will back its work. For example, the Mag-Lite carries a limited lifetime warranty. That's about as good as you will be offered. If the flashlight doesn't carry a solid guarantee or warranty, then select one that does carry it.

In summary, I hope that the above questions have helped you to think more clearly and more systematically about your forthcoming purchase. Possibly, too, they have helped you to more clearly identify the characteristics of your current flashlight.

As a further aid, the following checklist should help you in the selection of a flashlight which best meets your needs. Best of luck.

FLASHLIGHT CHECKLIST

A. The Flashlight Design

	Yes	No
1. Does the flashlight reflect light?	☐	☐
2. Does the flashlight contain a spare bulb?	☐	☐
3. Does the flashlight fit into your ring carrier?	☐	☐
4. Does the flashlight have a lexan lens?	☐	☐
5. Does the flashlight have any sharp edges?	☐	☐
6. Does the flashlight design make battery changing easy?	☐	☐
7. Does the flashlight design allow the light beam to be adjusted from spotlight to floodlight?	☐	☐
8. Does the flashlight design allow for it to be mounted in your vehicle?	☐	☐
9. Does the design of the flashlight switch assembly allow for smooth rolling of the flashlight?	☐	☐

	Yes	No
10. Does the style of flashlight come in various sizes?	☐	☐
11. Is the flashlight part of a family of flashlights?	☐	☐
12. Is the barrel of the flashlight made of heavy duty metal such as aircraft aluminum?	☐	☐
13. Is the barrel of the flashlight made of high-impact plastic?	☐	☐
14. Is the barrel of the flashlight made of plastic?	☐	☐
15. Is the barrel of the flashlight smooth?	☐	☐
16. Is the barrel of the flashlight knurled for better gripping?	☐	☐
17. Is the tail cap flat on the end?	☐	☐
18. Is the flashlight waterproof?	☐	☐
19. Is the flashlight explosion proof?	☐	☐
20. Is the flashlight easy to operate?	☐	☐
21. Is the flashlight rechargeable?	☐	☐
22. Is the flashlight easy to carry?	☐	☐
23. Can the flashlight head be removed?	☐	☐
24. Can the flashlight tail cap be removed?	☐	☐
25. Can the flashlight be easily concealed?	☐	☐
26. Will the flashlight break or crack if dropped on a hard surface?	☐	☐
27. Will the flashlight float if dropped into the water?	☐	☐
28. How much does the flashlight weigh?	☐	☐

B. The Flashlight On-Off Switch

	Yes	No
29. Does the flashlight have a slide-button on-off switch?	☐	☐
30. Does the flashlight have a push-button on-off switch?	☐	☐
31. Does the flashlight on-off switch let you blink the light?	☐	☐
32. Is the on-off switch easy to operate?	☐	☐
33. Is the on-off switch designed to withstand heavy usage?	☐	☐
34. Is the on-off switch designed to keep out dirt and foreign particles?	☐	☐
35. Is the on-off switch designed so that you can easily roll the flashlight across a smooth surface?	☐	☐
36. Will the on-off switch design hinder you in the using of the flashlight defensive control and restraint techniques?	☐	☐

C. The Flashlight Bulb

	Yes	No
37. Does the flashlight use a standard bulb?	☐	☐
38. Does the flashlight use a high-intensity bulb?	☐	☐
39. Can the bulb be easily purchased?	☐	☐
40. Can the bulb be easily changed?	☐	☐
41. What is the candlepower of the bulb?	☐	☐
42. Is the candlepower of the flashlight bulb over 30,000?	☐	☐
43. What is the service life of the bulb?	☐	☐
44. What is the average life of the bulb?	☐	☐
45. Does the bulb produce a bright, white light?	☐	☐

D. The Flashlight Battery

	Yes	No
46. Does the flashlight use standard batteries?	☐	☐
47. Does the flashlight use C-cell size batteries?	☐	☐
48. Does the flashlight use D-cell size batteries?	☐	☐
49. Does the flashlight use cartridge-type batteries?	☐	☐
50. Does the flashlight use rechargeable batteries?	☐	☐
51. Can the batteries be easily purchased?	☐	☐
52. Can the batteries be easily inserted?	☐	☐
53. Can the batteries be easily removed?	☐	☐
54. What is the discharge capacity of the battery?	☐	☐
55. What is the rated capacity of the battery?	☐	☐

E. The Rechargeable Flashlight

	Yes	No
56. Can you justify the purchase of a rechargeable flashlight?	☐	☐
57. Can the charger unit be used at home?	☐	☐
58. Can the charger unit be mounted in any position?	☐	☐
59. Can the charger unit be installed easily, quickly and economically?	☐	☐
60. Can your current flashlight be easily converted into a rechargeable one?	☐	☐
61. Does the charger unit have a charging-indicator light to show you when it's on?	☐	☐

	Yes	No
62. Does the rechargeable flashlight use a standard bulb?	☐	☐
63. What type of batteries must be used in the flashlight?	☐	☐
64. What is the "on-time" per charge?	☐	☐
65. What is the "track record" of the charger system?	☐	☐

F. The Accessories

	Yes	No
66. Can accessories be added to the flashlight?	☐	☐
67. Can traffic wands be easily attached to the flashlight head?	☐	☐

G. The Manufacturer

	Yes	No
68. Is the flashlight made by a well-known and reputable manufacturer?	☐	☐
69. What guarantee or warranty does the manufacturer give its flashlight?	☐	☐

Chapter III

PERSONAL WEAPONS

In addition to the weapons issued to you by the department, you also possess many personal weapons which can be used to help defend you during a confrontation. Your personal weapons include your head, your elbow, forearm, your hands and fingers, your knee and your foot.

Personal weapons are generally used when a firearm, a baton or a chemical agent cannot be used (e.g., crowded store, bus, etc.); when you do not have your firearm, baton or chemical agent (e.g., you've been taken hostage, or you're off duty); or when you are suddenly attacked, finding yourself unable to obtain your firearm, baton or chemical agent (e.g., you are jumped from behind, or you are unexpectedly attacked).

Your personal weapons and how they are used are described below. Learn how to use them, so that they can aid you in successfully defending yourself.

HEAD. If grabbed from the front or rear, forcefully smash your head into the attacker's face. Striking the attacker on the nose, lips, eyes and so forth should make him/her release his/her grip allowing you to use an appropriate defensive tactics technique.

ELBOW. If grabbed or choked from the rear, forcefully strike the person with the flat section of your elbow (it's just above the elbow at the base of your bicep). DO NOT USE THE TIP OF THE JOINT OF THE ELBOW AS THE ELBOW MAY BREAK. An elbow strike may be delivered to the person's head, chest, stomach, rib, abdominal and leg areas.

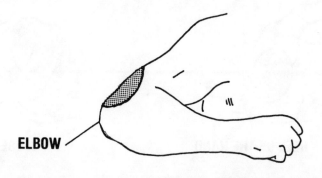

ELBOW

HANDS AND FINGERS. The fleshy edge of your hand can be used to "chop" or to strike the person. You can use the edge of your hand or fist to strike the person's head, shoulder, chest, arm, rib, stomach, abdominal or joint areas. The palm of your hand can also be used to strike these areas. Your fingers can be used to grasp the person's body, or to thrust into the person's eyes to temporarily blind him/her so that you can escape or use an appropriate defensive tactics movement.

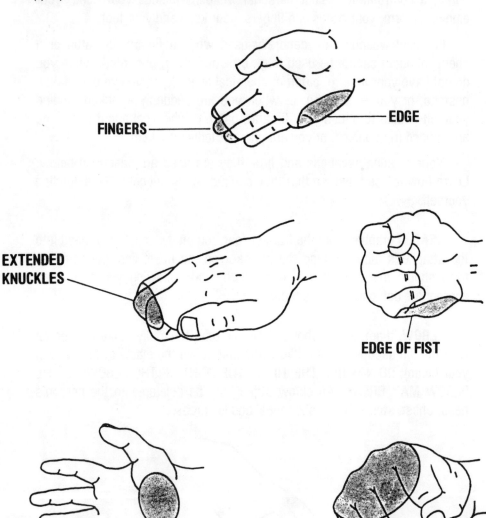

FINGERS

EDGE

EXTENDED KNUCKLES

EDGE OF FIST

HEEL OF THE HAND

CLOSED FIST

FOREARM. The meaty portion of your forearm can be used to block punches or similar type blows. You can also use it to strike a person in the head, shoulder, chest, rib and abdominal areas.

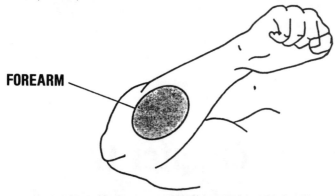

FOREARM

KNEE. The top of your knee (just above the knee joint) can be used to forcefully strike a person in almost any part of the body. DO NOT USE THE FRONT OR THE HINGED SECTION OF THE KNEE AS IT MAY BE BROKEN.

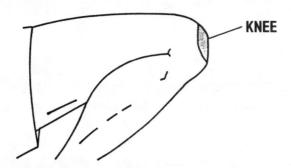

KNEE

FOOT. You can use the heel of your foot to stomp on a person's foot, or use your foot (shoe) to kick the person on the shin area. In most cases, these actions will cause the person to release his/her grip.

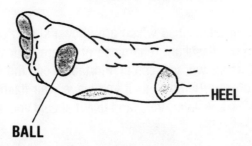

HEEL

BALL

Chapter IV

HOLDING AND CARRYING THE FLASHLIGHT

This section focuses upon the holding of and the carrying of the flashlight. As shown, there are two basic ways to hold the flashlight: civilian-style and police-style.

There is a growing trend among police officers to use the civilian-style grip. The reasons: it's more versatile; it's easier to use; and it reduces the temptation to strike the violator above his/her shoulder area.

For those who were wondering, the civilian-style grip is based upon the way a civilian normally picks up a flashlight.

The carrying techniques which are shown should enable you to carry and to reach your flashlight regardless of where your other equipment is located. Also, as shown, you can comfortably keep the flashlight in its belt carrier while driving. Remember, if you leave your flashlight in the cruiser while confronting a violator, you can't use it should you need it.

To hold the flashlight civilian-style simply grasp the barrel of the flashlight with your right hand behind its head. To keep a low profile hold the flashlight beside your leg.

Holding the flashlight civilian-style. Simply grasp the barrel of the flashlight with your right hand so that its head is pointing away from you.

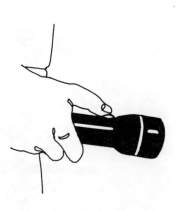

A close-up showing how the thumb is used to switch on/off this flashlight. This flashlight is a MAG-LITE which has a flush sealed rubber thumb button.

Holding the flashlight police-style. Simply grasp the barrel of the flashlight with your weak hand--palm up. Next, bend your weak arm at the elbow so that the barrel of the flashlight is shoulder height, and so its head is pointing away from you. To turn the flashlight on or off, simply press the button with either your middle or index finger.

View showing the flashlight ring on the weak side.

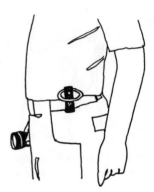

View showing the inverted flashlight ring position. Inverting the ring should raise your flashlight higher than your other equipment, with the exception of your radio. Hence, your flashlight should be easier to remove from the ring.

View showing how the flashlight is worn on the weak side.

Driving with your flashlight in its ring. Simply point the flashlight tail cap toward the brake. This should place the barrel of the flashlight on the seat and also place it parallel to your leg.

Chapter V

FLASHLIGHT RETENTION TECHNIQUES

This section focuses upon your retaining control of the flashlight. It was suggested by the manuscript reviewers at Calibre Press, Inc. that these techniques be presented in the beginning of the book. A check with other reviewers supported this belief. The reasons: the learning of retention techniques should enable you to keep your flashlight, even if someone should grasp it during the application of a defensive technique; the learning of retention techniques should ease your nerves about the "what should I do now?" syndrome, should the violator grasp your flashlight, in an attempt to take it; and the learning of retention techniques should boost your confidence in the use of the flashlight techniques which are presented in this book. After analyzing the reviewers' comments, I agree with them. Herewith, the retention techniques.

SITUATION: A person grabs the barrel of your flashlight with his/her right hand.

ACTION:

1

Standing in the interrogation position (firearm away from the person) you are holding the flashlight by the barrel in your right hand. You grip the flashlight at the base of its head so the tail cap is pointing forward. During the conversation with the person, you move the flashlight forward when making a gesture with your right hand. Suddenly, the person grabs the barrel of the flashlight with his/her right hand. The person's right hand is located toward the tail cap section of the barrel.

2

Quickly grasp the barrel with your left hand.

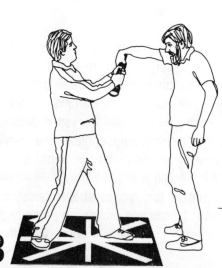

3

Keeping both of your hands on the barrel, rotate your hands and the barrel in a small semi-circular clockwise motion. Notice how the person's right wrist will bend as the tail cap is pointed upward.

4

A close-up view showing how the tail cap portion of the barrel is rotated clockwise over the person's wrist.

5 Continue the clockwise motion until the person's hand is palm-up and the barrel is on top of the person's right wrist. Forcefully, push the tail cap portion of the barrel downward and against the person's wrist.

6 This action should pull the barrel upward freeing it from the person's right thumb and fingers. Use appropriate follow-up measures.

SITUATION: A person grabs the barrel of your flashlight with his/her right hand.

ACTION:

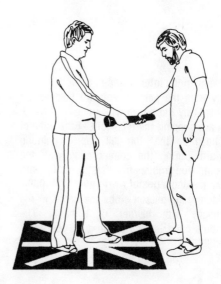

1 Standing in the interrogation position (firearm away from the person) you are holding the flashlight by the barrel with your right hand. You are gripping the flashlight at the base of its head so that the tail cap is pointing forward. During the conversation with the person, you move the flashlight forward when making a gesture with your right hand. Suddenly, the person grabs the barrel of the flashlight with his/her right hand.

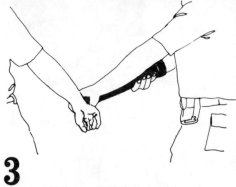

2

Immediately, grasp the tail cap portion of the barrel with your left hand. Quickly, rotate the flashlight in a clockwise direction by lifting upward and pushing to your right with your left hand; simultaneously, push downward and to your left with your right hand.

3

Continue the clockwise rotation until the flashlight is released by the person. Use appropriate follow-up measures.

SITUATION: A person grabs the barrel of your flashlight with his/her right hand.

ACTION:

1

Standing in the interrogation position (firearm away from the person) you are holding the flashlight by the barrel with your right hand. You are gripping the flashlight at the base of its head so that the tail cap is pointing forward. During the conversation with the person, you move the flashlight forward when making a gesture with your right hand. Suddenly, the person grabs the barrel of the flashlight with his/her right hand. The person's hand is located next to your right hand.

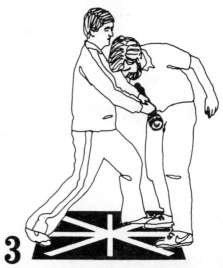

2

Immediately, grasp the tail cap portion of the flashlight barrel with your left hand. The palm of your left hand should be placed under the barrel for better control of the flashlight during the use of this defensive retention technique.

3

Force the person's right arm to bend at the elbow by stepping forward and to the left with your left leg. Keep your balance by placing your left foot next to the person's right foot. Simultaneously, bend your left arm at the elbow while pushing downward on the barrel with your right arm. This action should forcefully push the head of the flashlight into the person's stomach, lower abdominal or groin area causing him/her to release the flashlight. Use appropriate follow-up measures.

SITUATION: A person grabs the barrel of your flashlight with his/her right hand.

ACTION:

1

Standing in the interrogation position (firearm away from the person) you are holding the flashlight by the barrel with your right hand. You are gripping the flashlight at the base of its head so that the tail cap is pointing forward. During the conversation with the person, you move the flashlight forward when making a gesture with your right hand. Suddenly, the person grabs the barrel of the flashlight with his/her right hand. Immediately grasp the barrel of the flashlight with your left hand--palm down.

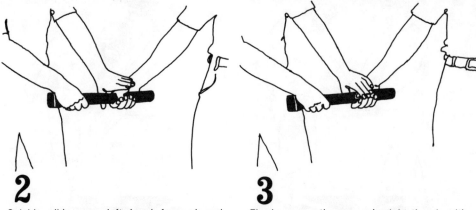

2

Quickly slide your left hand forward and toward the person's hand. As you slide your left hand forward open it placing your fingers over the person's right thumb.

3

Firmly, grasp the person's right thumb with your left hand. Begin to roll the person's thumb into the barrel of the flashlight. The reason: you want to create pain by rolling the person's thumb into the barrel. Simultaneously, squeeze the person's thumb bone against the barrel. This action should create intense pain.

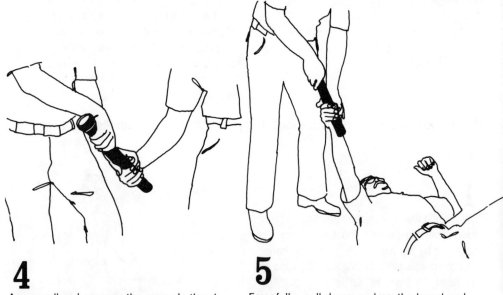

4

As you roll and squeeze the person's thumb, lift upward upon the head of the flashlight. This action should make the person's balance shift to his/her right side, while causing his/her knees to bend.

5

Forcefully, pull downward on the barrel and the person's thumb with your left hand. Simultaneously make a quarter turn by stepping backward with your left leg. This action should cause the person to lie upon the ground. To insure pain compliance, keep pressure firmly against the person's thumb.

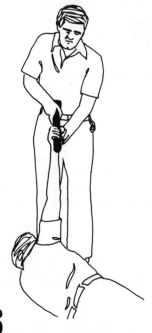

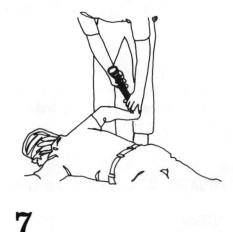

6

After the person is lying upon the ground, keep the person's arm straight by pulling upward on the flashlight. To roll the person onto his/her stomach for handcuffing, begin walking to your left. As you walk, keep the person's arm straight by pulling upward.

7

After the person is on his/her stomach, bend the person's right arm at the elbow.

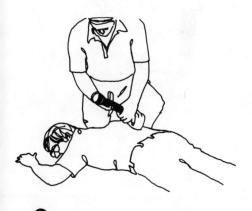

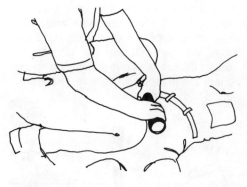

8

Kneel upon the person's right shoulder at a 45° angle with your right knee. You may now handcuff the person or use other appropriate follow-up measures.

9

A close-up view showing the proper placement of your right knee.

Chapter VI

BASIC DEFENSIVE BLOCKING TECHNIQUES USING A FLASHLIGHT

This section focuses upon the use of the flashlight to supplement your basic blocking abilities. Using the flashlight as shown in this chapter should make your blocks stronger and thus more effective. This should result in less injury to you.

SITUATION: While talking to a person, (s)he attempts to punch you in the face.

ACTION:

1

Suddenly, the person attempts to punch you in the face with his/her right hand. Quickly, bend your right arm at the elbow so that the head of the flashlight is pointing upward. Holding the barrel tightly against your right forearm, swiftly thrust your right arm across your body so the barrel of the flashlight strikes the person's right forearm. Keep the flashlight on a slight downward angle and step into the person while stepping backward with your left leg. The reasons: to deflect the punch, to give you more blocking power and to keep your balance. Use appropriate follow-up measures.

2

A view from your right showing how the block is made with the barrel of the flashlight.

SITUATION: While talking to a person, (s)he attempts to punch you in the face with his/her left hand.

ACTION:

1

Standing in the interrogation position, (firearm away from the person) and holding the flashlight civilian-style in your right hand, you begin talking to the person.

2

Suddenly, the person attempts to punch you in the face with his/her left hand. Quickly, bend your right arm at the elbow so that the head of the flashlight is pointing upward. Holding the barrel tightly against your right forearm, swiftly thrust your right arm outward so the barrel of the flashlight strikes the person's left forearm. Keep the flashlight on a slight downward angle and step into the person while stepping backward with your right leg. The reasons: to deflect the punch, to give you more blocking power, and to keep your balance. Use appropriate follow-up measures.

3

A view from your left showing how the block is made with the barrel of the flashlight.

SITUATION: A person attempts to hit you with a club in an over-the-head manner.

ACTION:

1

Standing in the interrogation position (firearm away from the person) and holding the flashlight civilian-style in your right hand, you begin talking to the person.

2

As the person raises the club, quickly raise your right arm so that your forearm is above, but in front of, your forehead. Holding the barrel tightly against your forearm, step into the attack while thrusting the barrel toward the club. The reasons: to block and to "stuff" the attack. Also, keep your right arm on an angle so that upon impact, the club will be deflected toward the ground. Use appropriate follow-up measures.

NOTE: Keep the flashlight in front of and above your head. The reason: to reduce the possibility of the club hitting you on the head or in the face. Also, make sure that the club impacts upon the barrel. The reason: so that you do not get broken fingers.

SITUATION: While talking to a person, (s)he attempts to hit you in the chest area with a club.

ACTION:

1

Standing in the interrogation position (firearm away from the person) and holding the flashlight civilian-style in your left hand, you begin talking to a person.

2

Suddenly, the person attempts to hit you in the chest area with a club. As the person starts to swing the club, move your left arm forward bending it at the elbow, so that the tail cap portion of the barrel is pointing toward the ground. Quickly grasp the tail cap portion of the barrel with your right hand.

3

Having grasped the flashlight at both ends, forcefully push the vertically-held barrel into the oncoming club. If possible, step into the attack. The reasons: to "stuff" and to block the attack. Use appropriate follow-up measures.

SITUATION: While talking to a person, (s)he attempts to hit the right side of your rib cage with a club.

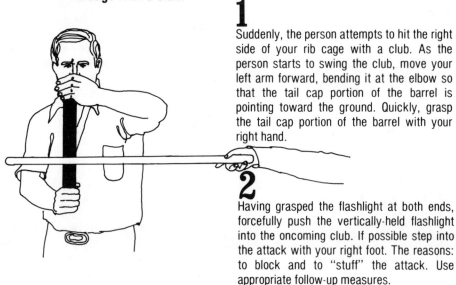

1

Suddenly, the person attempts to hit the right side of your rib cage with a club. As the person starts to swing the club, move your left arm forward, bending it at the elbow so that the tail cap portion of the barrel is pointing toward the ground. Quickly, grasp the tail cap portion of the barrel with your right hand.

2

Having grasped the flashlight at both ends, forcefully push the vertically-held flashlight into the oncoming club. If possible step into the attack with your right foot. The reasons: to block and to "stuff" the attack. Use appropriate follow-up measures.

SITUATION: While talking to a person, (s)he attempts to hit the left side of your rib cage with a club.

ACTION:

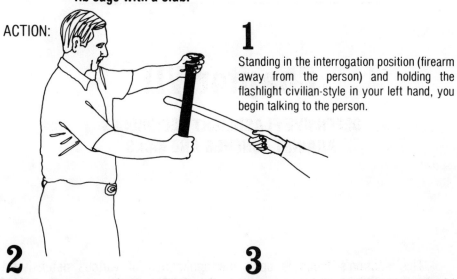

1

Standing in the interrogation position (firearm away from the person) and holding the flashlight civilian-style in your left hand, you begin talking to the person.

2

Suddenly, the person attempts to hit the left side of your rib cage with a club. As the person starts to swing the club, move your left arm forward, bending it at the elbow so that the tail cap portion of the barrel is pointing toward the ground. Quickly, grasp the tail cap portion of the barrel with your right hand.

3

Having grasped the flashlight at both ends, forcefully push the vertically-held flashlight into the oncoming club. If possible, step into the attack with your left foot. The reasons: to block and to "stuff" the attack. Use appropriate follow-up measures.

SITUATION: A person attempts to hit you with a club in an over-the-head manner.

ACTION:

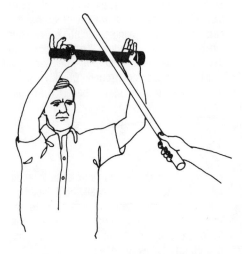

1

Standing in the interrogation position (firearm away from the person) and holding the flashlight civilian-style in your right hand, you begin talking to the person.

2

Suddenly, the person, who is holding a club in his/her right hand, raises it to hit you. As the person raises his/her arm, swing the flashlight in front of you and to the left. Grasp the head with your left hand when it is in front of your left shoulder. Next, using both of your arms, forcefully thrust the horizontally-held flashlight upward, away from you and toward the club. If possible, step into the attack. The reasons: to block and to "stuff" the attack. Use appropriate follow-up measures.

Chapter VII

DEFENSIVE FLASHLIGHT TECHNIQUES AGAINST PUNCHES AND KICKS

This section's focus is upon the application of various defensive techniques which you may use should the violator attempt to punch or to kick at you. Remember to practice these defensive techniques, since your speed, most likely, will be a factor in the successful application of these techniques.

SITUATION: While talking to a person, (s)he attempts to punch you in the face.

ACTION:

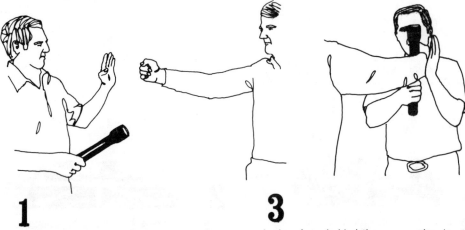

1

Suddenly, the person attempts to punch you in the face with his/her right hand. As (s)he begins to punch, lean back. Simultaneously, thrust your left arm--hand open, fingers together--forward, while sliding your hand toward the tail cap portion of the flashlight.

3

A view from behind the person showing the sandwiching of his/her right wrist. Use appropriate follow-up measures.

NOTE: There is a possibility that the person's right wrist may be broken upon its coming into contact with the flashlight.

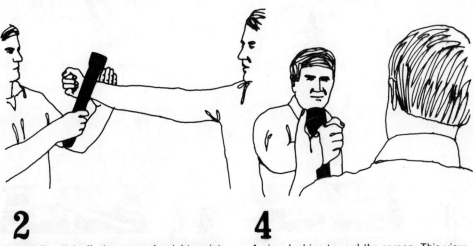

2

Forcefully, "slap" the person's right wrist with both your left hand and the flashlight. This action is similar to clapping your hands together only here, the person's wrist is being sandwiched between your left wrist and the flashlight.

4

A view looking toward the person. This view shows the proper positioning of your left hand.

SITUATION: While talking to a person, (s)he attempts to punch you in the face.

ACTION:

1
Standing in the interrogation position--firearm away from the person--and holding the flashlight by its barrel at shoulder height, you begin talking to the person.

2
Suddenly, the person attempts to punch you in the face with his/her right hand. As (s)he begins to punch, lean back and to the right. The reasons: to increase the distance between you and the punch, and to also properly position yourself for a defensive response.

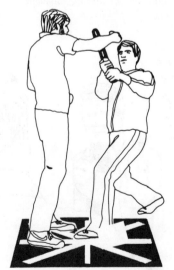

3
Simultaneously, grasp the head of the flashlight with your left hand. Snap the flashlight in a quasi 45° arc striking the person's right forearm or wrist with the barrel. This action should block the person's punch.

4
A view from the right side showing the blocking of the person's punch. Use appropriate follow-up measures.

NOTE: There is a possibility that the person's right wrist may be broken upon its coming into contact with the barrel of the flashlight.

SITUATION: While talking to a person, (s)he attempts to punch you in the face using a "one-two" combination.

ACTION:

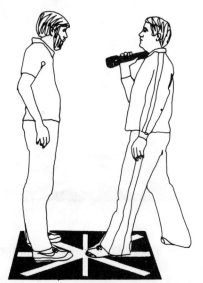

1

Standing in the interrogation position--firearm away from the person--while holding the flashlight--police-style--, you begin talking to the person.

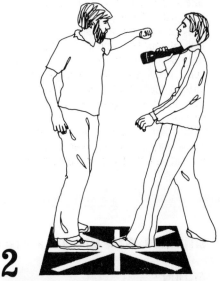

2

Suddenly, the person attempts to punch you in the face with his/her left hand. As (s)he begins to punch, lean backwards and to the right. The reasons: to slightly increase the distance between you and the punch, and to also position yourself for your defensive response.

3

Simultaneously, grasp the head of the flashlight with your left hand. Snap the flashlight forward and to the right striking the person's left forearm or wrist with the barrel. Keep your balance by slightly pivoting to the right on the balls of your feet, and by turning your upper body slightly to the right.

4

After blocking the person's left punch, (s)he attempts to punch you in the face with the right hand. Quickly, shift your balance and body position by pivoting to the left on the balls of your feet, and by turning your upper body slightly to the left. As you turn your upper body, snap the flashlight to the left striking the person's right forearm or wrist with the barrel. Use appropriate follow-up measures.

NOTE: There is a possibility that the person's wrists may be broken when they come into contact with the barrel of the flashlight.

SITUATION: While talking to a person, (s)he attempts to punch you in the face.

ACTION:

1

Suddenly, the person attempts to punch you in the face with his/her right hand. As (s)he begins to punch, lean back and to the right. The reasons: to increase the distance between you and the punch, and to also properly position yourself for a defensive response.

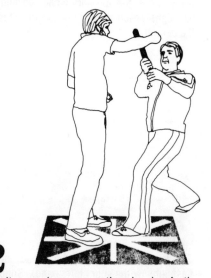

2

Simultaneously, grasp the head of the flashlight with your left hand. Snap the flashlight in a quasi 45º arc striking the person's right forearm or wrist with the barrel. This action should block the person's punch.

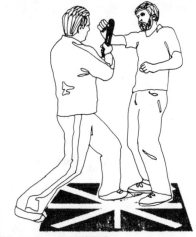

3

A view from the right side showing the blocking of the person's punch.

If the person is on drugs, alcohol or is mentally unstable and continues to attack you after blocking his/her punch (no pain is felt) here are a few follow-up defensive combination techniques.

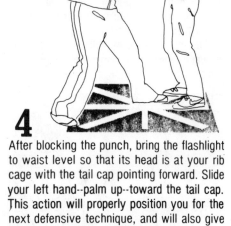

4

After blocking the punch, bring the flashlight to waist level so that its head is at your rib cage with the tail cap pointing forward. Slide your left hand--palm up--toward the tail cap. This action will properly position you for the next defensive technique, and will also give you better control of the flashlight.

5

Forcefully, push the tail cap into the person's stomach or lower abdominal area by thrusting your arms forward and in a straight line. For extra power, slightly twist your hips to the left and slightly bend your left knee.

NOTE: Do not strike the person in the solar plexus. The reason: you could rupture the spleen causing death.

6

After pushing the tail cap into the person's stomach or lower abdominal area, slightly pull back both of your arms so the tail cap is an inch or two away from the person. Next, bend your left arm at the elbow while simultaneously pushing downward on the barrel with your right arm. This action should forcefully push the head of the flashlight into the person's lower abdominal or groin area causing him/her to stop fighting. Use appropriate follow-up measures.

SITUATION: A person attempts to kick you in the groin.

ACTION:

1

Standing in the interrogation position (firearm away from the person), you begin talking to the person. You are holding the flashlight in the "on-guard" position. That is, you are holding the flashlight by both ends (one hand on each end) in a horizontal, waist-level position.

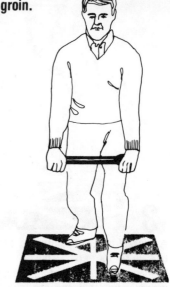

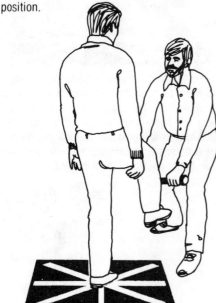

2

Suddenly the person lifts his/her right foot in an attempt to kick you in the groin area. Immediately, thrust your right leg backward. The reasons: to move your groin area away from the kick; to move your firearm farther away; and to keep your balance. Simultaneously, with both of your arms, forcefully thrust the horizontally-held flashlight downward, away from you and toward the person's right shin. The reasons: to block and to "stuff" the kick.

NOTE: Keep your eyes on the person and your back straight as possible. The reasons: The kick could be a fake, hence (s)he could punch you in the face. Keeping your back straight will also help to keep you from leaning forward-- possibly into the punch. Finally, keeping your eyes on the suspect lets you see if (s)he has pulled a gun or a knife.

3

A close-up view showing the blocking of the kick using the barrel of the flashlight. Attempt to block the kick with the barrel, not with your fingers. The reason: the kick could break your fingers. Use appropriate follow-up measures.

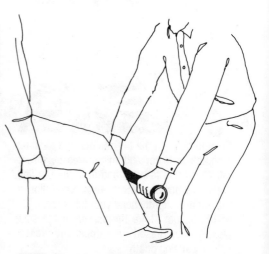

NOTE: There is a possibility that the person's right shin may be broken upon its coming into contact with the barrel.

SITUATION: A person attempts to kick you in the groin.

ACTION:

1

Standing in the interrogation position (firearm away from the person), you begin talking to the person. You are holding the flashlight in the "on-guard" position. That is, you are holding the flashlight by both hands (one hand on each end) in a horizontal, waist-level position.

2

Suddenly, the person lifts his/her right foot in an attempt to kick you in the groin area. Immediately thrust your left leg backward. The reasons: to move your groin area away from the kick; and to keep your balance. Simultaneously, snap the flashlight in a quasi 45⁰ downward arc striking the person's right shin with the barrel. This action should block the person's kick. Use appropriate follow-up measures.

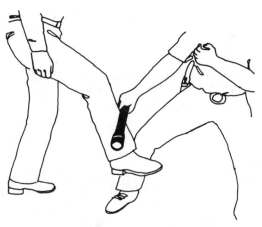

NOTE: There is a possibility that the person's right shin may be broken upon coming into contact with the barrel.

Chapter VIII

CONTROL AND RESTRAINT: DEFENSIVE FLASHLIGHT TECHNIQUES

The controlling of an individual through the use of simple, effective, safe and socially acceptable techniques is the focus of this section. While there are many controlling and restraining techniques, the ones selected for this chapter should be easy to learn and easy to retain after a few short practice sessions.

When you are practicing the techniques which are shown, attempt to combine the various control and restraint holds. You will want to develop versatility with these techniques so that you can adapt to the violator's changes in strategy or in movement.

SITUATION: After advising the person that (s)he must go with you, (s)he refuses and begins to walk away.

ACTION:

1

Standing behind the person you advise him/her that (s)he must go with you. (S)He refuses and begins to walk away.

2

Staying to the rear of the person for safety reasons, grasp the person's right wrist with your left hand. Simultaneously, move the barrel of the flashlight toward the person's right wrist. **NOTE:** Your weak leg is forward which helps you to maintain balance, while also keeping your firearm farther away from the person. Also, keep to the side of the person. The reasons: to avoid being kicked, and for ease in the application of the technique.

3

Having grasped the person's right wrist, quickly place the barrel of the flashlight over the person's right radial (top wrist) bone.

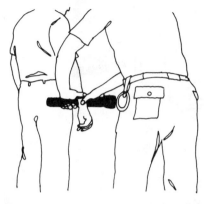

4

A view from behind the person showing proper thumb placement.

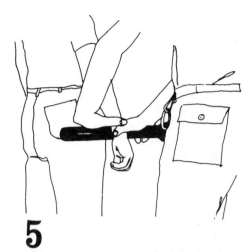

5

A close-up view showing proper placement of the thumbs and of the barrel of the flashlight.

6

Quickly grasp the barrel of the flashlight with both of your hands. Simultaneously place both of your thumbs under the person's wrist. The web of your hands (the skin between your thumbs and index fingers) must be held tightly against each side of the person's right wrist. The reason: to keep the flashlight stable.

7

Forcefully squeeze the flashlight against the person's radial (top wrist) bone, while slightly rotating the flashlight toward the person's hand. This movement should cause pain while also making the person's knees bend, causing him/her to bend forward at the waist. Rember to maintain pressure on the person's wrist for pain compliance.

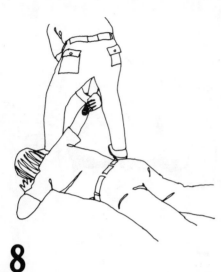

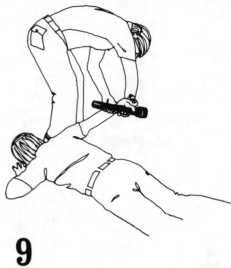

8

After the person is upon the ground--face down--step over the person's right arm with your left leg. Keep firm pressure on the person's radial (top wrist) bone with the barrel of the flashlight. The reasons: to keep control of the person's arm, and to maintain pain compliance.

9

Keeping firm pressure on the person's radial (top wrist) bone with the barrel, step over the person's right arm with your right leg.

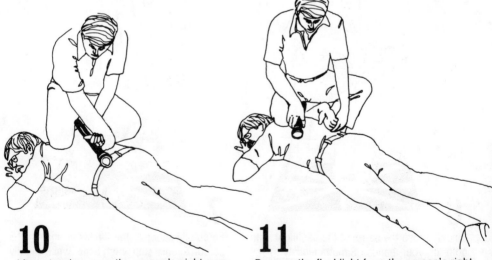

10

After stepping over the person's right arm, bend his/her arm at the elbow, and kneel on his/her right shoulder. Your right knee is placed diagonally across his/her right shoulder blade. Your left leg "traps" the person's left arm.

11

Remove the flashlight from the person's right wrist, while grasping his/her right fingers with your left hand. Hyper-extend the fingers to raise the wrist for handcuffing. Be careful not to injure the person's fingers. Use appropriate follow-up measures.

SITUATION: While talking to a person, (s)he grabs your shirt.

ACTION:

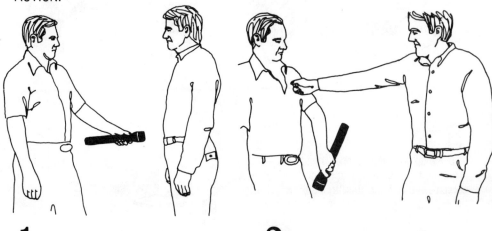

1

Standing in the interrogation position (firearm away from the person) and holding the flashlight civilian-style, you begin talking to the person.

2

Suddenly, the person grabs your shirt or badge with his/her right hand. Immediately, rotate your left arm so that the head of the flashlight is pointing toward the ground.

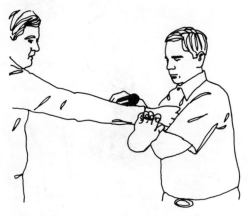

3

Raise your left hand by bending your arm at the elbow. Place the barrel over the person's right wrist area. As you place the barrel over the person's wrist--tail cap to your left-- prepare to grasp the tail cap portion of the barrel with your left hand.

4

Grasp the tail cap portion of the barrel with your left hand. Slide your left hand as close to the person's wrist as possible to insure a tight grip. For ease in grasping the tail cap portion of the barrel, reach under and in front of your left forearm with your right arm.

5

A close-up showing proper hand and arm placement. To insure a tight lock over the person's wrist, keep the "triangle" which is formed between your forearms and the barrel as small as possible.

6

After "locking" the flashlight into place, step back with your left foot, while pulling downward and to your left on the flashlight. This action should cause the person's right knee to bend and cause him/her to bend forward at the waist.

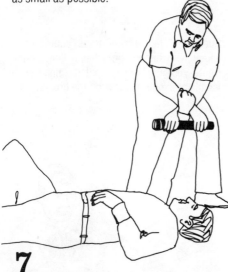

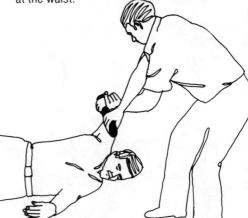

7

Keeping a snug "lock" on the person's wrist by tightly gripping the flashlight, pull his/her arm upward. Continue pulling downward on the flashlight until the person falls to the ground. The quarter turn movement with your left leg should cause the person to land on his/her back. Keeping the snug "lock" on the person's wrist by tightly gripping the flashlight, pull him/her upward until the elbow is straight. The reason: this action will aid in rolling the person onto his/her stomach for handcuffing.

8

Keeping your tight lock on the person's wrist, begin to walk around his/her head. As you walk, pull upward to keep the person's arm straight. This action should cause the person to roll onto his/her side as shown.

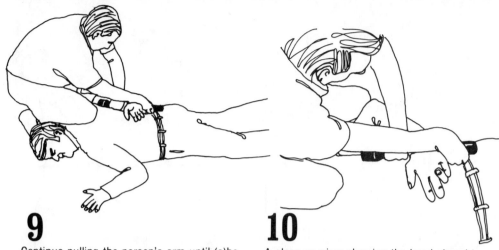

9

Continue pulling the person's arm until (s)he has rolled onto his/her stomach. Immediately, bend the person's right arm at the elbow, placing his/her hand on the small of the back. Kneel upon the person's shoulder at a 45° angle with your right knee. You may now handcuff the person or use other appropriate follow-up measures.

10

A close-up view showing the hand placed in the small of the back.

SITUATION: As a person begins to enter a doorway, (s)he suddenly braces against the doorjamb using both of his/her arms refusing to move.

ACTION:

1

As a person begins to enter a doorway, (s)he suddenly braces against the doorjamb using both of his/her arms, refusing to move.

2

Holding the barrel of the flashlight in your strong hand, approach the person from your non-firearm side. The reason: to avoid being kicked or having your gun snatched. Your weak hand should be directly under the person's right forearm in preparation for grasping the barrel of the flashlight.

3

Place the barrel of the flashlight over the person's right radial (top wrist) bone. Simultaneously, reach under the person's right forearm with your weak hand, grasping the barrel of the flashlight on the inside of the person's right wrist. Place both of your thumbs under the person's wrist. The web of your hands (the skin between your thumbs and index fingers) must be held tightly against each side of the person's right wrist. The reason: to keep the flashlight stable.

5

Rather than clamp the radial (top wrist) bone with the barrel of the flashlight, you may wish to place the flashlight between the person's legs. To do so, push one end of the flashlight between the person's legs. Then, turn the flashlight so that it is horizontal, make sure that the palm of your hand is under the flashlight. The reason: the chances of your arm or elbow being broken should the person suddenly squat are greatly reduced.

To move the person, simply bend your right arm at the elbow forcing your wrist area into the person's groin area. To help the person keep his/her balance, grasp the shirt and/or coat collar. If the person is not wearing a shirt, grasp the hair or the ear. The uncomfortable feeling which is produced should enable you to move the person. Use appropriate follow-up techniques.

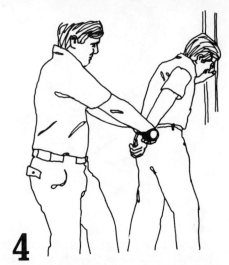

4

Forcefully, squeeze the flashlight tightly against the person's radial (top wrist) bone, while slightly rotating the flashlight toward the person's hand. Simultaneously, pull the person's right arm downward, toward your waist. You may now place the person onto the ground--face down--for handcuffing; walk them through the doorway; use other appropriate follow-up measures.

CAUTION: Smaller officers who try this technique may find difficulty in its application. The reasons: height, weight and strength differences.

Chapter IX

PASSIVE PERSONS:
DEFENSIVE FLASHLIGHT TECHNIQUES

This section focuses upon the passive person who may be lying, be standing or be sitting. Since the person is only passive, under most circumstances, the force that you may use to (re)move them must be minimal. You'll have a very difficult time trying to justify the striking of a person--in most circumstances--if (s)he is not offering any aggressive resistance. The techniques which are shown in this chapter are based upon (re)moving the passive violator via control, restraint and/or pain compliance.

SITUATION: A person who is lying on his/her back refuses to move when asked to stand or to leave.

ACTION:

1
Slowly approach the person on an angle to reduce the risk of being kicked. Generally, your approach will be made by walking toward the tip of the person's shoulder. As shown, the flashlight is being held in your strong hand, tail cap pointing downward.

2
Bending over the person's upper body, **push** the tail cap edge of the flashlight into the person's breast bone (upper chest) area. Keep pressure on this area until the person's hands and arms reach toward the flashlight.

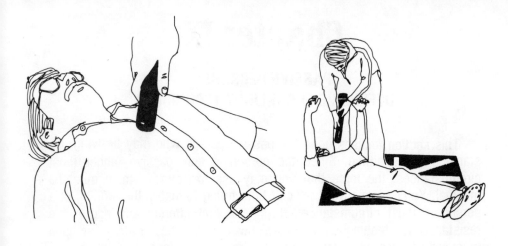

3

A close-up view showing how and where the edge of the tail cap is applied.

4

As the person's arms reach upward, remove the flashlight from the person's chest.

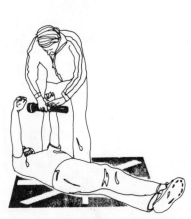

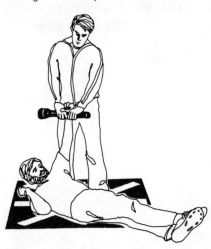

5

Quickly, place the barrel of the flashlight against the person's radial (top wrist) bone. Grasp the barrel of the flashlight with both of your hands. Simultaneously, place both of your thumbs over the person's wrist. The web of your hands (the skin between your thumbs and index fingers) must be held tightly against each side of the person's left wrist. The reason: to keep the flashlight stable.

Forcefully squeezing the flashlight against the person's radial (top wrist) bone, will move the person in the direction you wish. Should you desire to handcuff the individual, simply walk around the person's head, rolling him/her onto his/her stomach. Use appropriate follow-up measures.

SITUATION: After advising the person that (s)he must go along with you, (s)he refuses and stands motionless.

ACTION·

1

Standing alongside the person, you advise him/her that (s)he must go with you. (S)He refuses and stands motionless.

2

Holding the flashlight in your right hand near the base of its head, grasp the person's right wrist with your left hand. **NOTE:** Your weak leg is forward which helps you to maintain balance, while also keeping your firearm farther away from the person. Also, keep to the side of the person to avoid being kicked, and for ease in the technique application.

3

Lift the person's right arm so that it bends at the elbow. Also, trap the person's arm by placing his/her elbow between your left rib cage and your left forearm.

4

Quickly, raise the flashlight so that its tail cap is placed over the person's right arm. The tail cap of the flashlight must be pointing toward your left elbow for ease in the application of the technique.

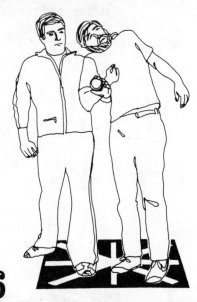

5

Push the barrel of the flashlight over the person's right forearm so that the tail cap is under your left tricep.

6

After the flashlight has been properly placed over the person's right arm, grasp the globe of the flashlight with your left hand. Pulling down on the head while simultaneously flexing the muscles in your left forearm should create pressure on the muscles and tendons of the person's right forearm. This pressure should create pain. You may now walk the person away with you or use the other appropriate follow-up measures.

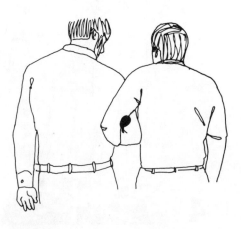

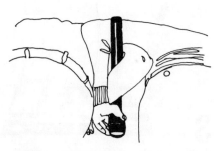

7

Rear view showing the proper placement of the tail cap and the barrel.

8

View looking upward showing the proper placement of the flashlight.

SITUATION: A person who is sitting on a chair, bar stool or similar piece of furniture refuses to move when you tell him/her to stand.

ACTION:

1

Holding the flashlight in your right hand behind its head approach the person who is sitting in the chair from either the right or left rear corner. The reasons: safety to you and to help keep him/her from seeing what you're doing. Notice that the person has grasped the sides of the chair seat with both hands. Keep your left hand on the chair to detect movement.

2

Keeping your left foot behind the chair for safety reasons, reach forward with your right hand. The flashlight should be placed in front of the person's right arm at approximately elbow height. This movement will make it easier for you to apply the technique.

3

Insert the tail cap portion of the flashlight between the person's right arm and his/her rib cage.

4

Having inserted the flashlight between the person's right arm and rib cage, grasp the tail cap end of the flashlight with your weak hand. Push the tail cap end of the flashlight forward and into the person's tricep area. The reason: to move him/her forward. Notice that your right hand is still holding the flashlight behind the globe.

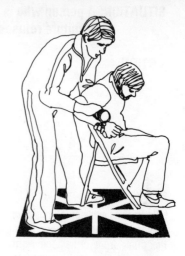

5

Quickly, pull the person's right hand from the chair seat, using your left hand. This can be done by grasping the person's right wrist-palm up--as shown. Bend the person's right arm at the elbow by pulling up on his/her wrist. Notice that the flashlight is placed in the crook of the person's right arm.

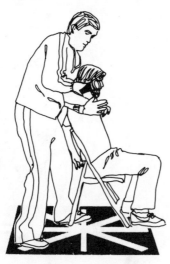

6

As you stand erect, push down upon the flashlight with your right hand. This pressure coupled with the keeping of the flashlight parallel to the ground should cause pain to the person's forearm area.

7

Begin to lift the person off the chair by simultaneously pushing down upon the globe of the flashlight with your right hand, while pulling upward on the person's right wrist with your left hand. After the person has been removed, use appropriate follow-up procedures.

SITUATION: A person who is sitting on a chair or on a similar piece of furniture refuses to move when you tell him/her to stand.

ACTION:

1

Holding the flashlight in your right hand behind its head, approach the person from behind. The reasons: safety to you and to help keep him/her from seeing what you're doing. Notice that the person's hands are on his/her legs.

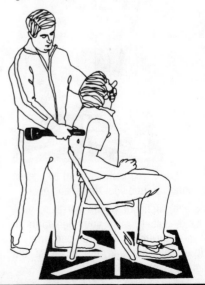

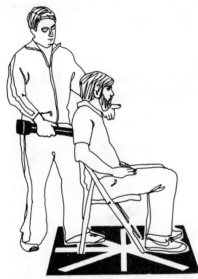

2

Simultaneously, cup the person's chin in the palm of your left hand, while placing the tail cap of the flashlight into the person's back. Place the tail cap of the flashlight against the person's back just above the top of the chair back. This location will ease in the application of this technique. **NOTE:** For safety reasons, do not place the flashlight against the person's spinal column.

3

Push the tail cap of the flashlight into the person's back while simultaneously pulling upward on the person's chin. These actions should remove the person from the chair. Once the person is standing, use appropriate follow-up procedures.

Chapter X

CHOKES:
DEFENSIVE FLASHLIGHT TECHNIQUES

This section contains numerous defensive flashlight escape techniques should you be choked by the violator. You should practice these defensive escape techniques until you can apply them without thinking. The reason: a choke can quickly render you unconscious, thus allowing the person to virtually do anything to you.

This section contains a selection of defensive techniques which can be used in various situations. Practice the ones that you like best. After all, you never know when you'll be called upon to use them.

SITUATION: You are being choked from the front by a person who has grasped you around the neck and the throat with both hands.

ACTION:

1

A person chokes you from the front by placing his/her hands around your throat and neck.

Holding the flashlight by its barrel in your right hand, quickly raise your right arm so that it is outstretched. Rotate your wrist so that it is palm up and the globe of the flashlight is pointing behind you.

2

Prepare to deliver a forceful strike to the person by "cocking" your right wrist.

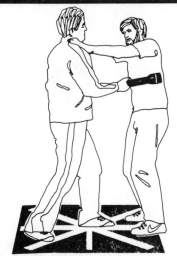

3

Forcefully snap your wrist forward. Simultaneously move your right arm in a horizontal arc so that the flashlight impacts against the person's left rib cage. The impact should make the person release the grip around your neck. Use appropriate follow-up procedures.

NOTE: Although the person has just tried to kill you, you still have a duty to help the person. This defensive escape technique should most likely, break the person's left knee or make it bend. Therefore, if necessary, give whatever medical treatment you are qualified to administer, and/or transport the person to the hospital.

4

You may also choose to strike the person on the side of his/her left knee. This may be done in lieu of striking the person in the rib cage, or be done as a follow-up move should the person not release the grasp around your neck. To strike the side of the knee, forcefully snap your wrist downward. Simultaneously, move your right arm in a downward arc so that the flashlight impacts against the side of the person's left knee. The impact should make the person release the grip around your neck. Use appropriate follow-up procedures.

SITUATION: You are being choked from the front by a person who has grasped you around the neck and the throat with both hands.

ACTION:

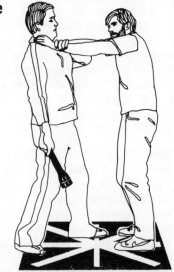

1

Immediately, grasp the person's left wrist by inserting your left hand between his/her arms. This action causes no injury or pain to the person. It is simply to hold the person's left arm so that it doesn't move.

2

Quickly, make a quarter turn by stepping backward with your left foot. This action should cause the person to lose balance, and cause his/her left elbow to rotate upward.

3

Next, raise the flashlight so that your arm is bent at the elbow, and the globe of the flashlight is approximately ear level. The reason: to properly position your arm and the flashlight to complete the defensive escape technique.

4

With your left hand, rotate the person's left arm so that his/her elbow is pointing upward. Forcefully, snap your wrist forward. Simultaneously, move your right arm in a downward arc so that the flashlight impacts against the area slightly above the person's left elbow. The impact should make the person release the grip around your neck. Use appropriate follow-up measures.

NOTE: Although the person has just tried to kill you, you still have a duty to help the person. This defensive escape technique should, most likely, break the person's left elbow. Therefore, if necessary give whatever medical treatment you are qualified to administer, and/or transport the person to the hospital.

SITUATION: You are talking to a person when (s)he suddenly begins to choke you, from the front, around the neck and the throat with both hands.

ACTION:

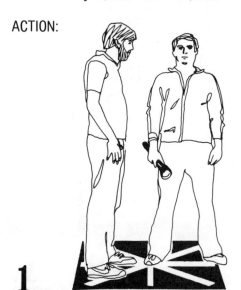

1 You are talking to a person so that only your side is facing his/her body.

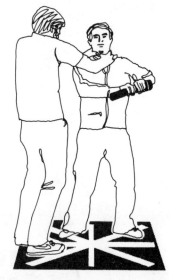

2 Suddenly, (s)he chokes you, from the front, around the neck and the throat with both hands. Quickly, move the flashlight across your body by bending your right elbow. Grasp the flashlight behind its head with your left hand--palm down. The reason: to properly position yourself and the flashlight to properly use a defensive escape technique.

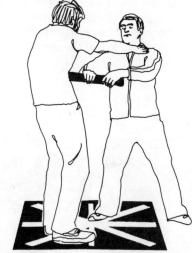

3 Forcefully, push the tail cap portion of the flashlight into the person's stomach area, by quickly pushing both of your arms toward his/her mid-section. **NOTE:** DO NOT push the flashlight into the person's solar plexus. The reasons: death or serious injury could result. This action should make the person release the grip around your neck. Use appropriate follow-up measures.

SITUATION: You are being choked from the front by a person who has grasped you around the neck and the throat with both hands.

ACTION:

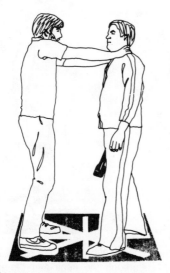

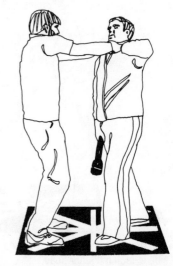

1 A person chokes you from the front by placing his/her hands around your throat and neck.

2 Quickly, raise your left arm and grasp the person's right wrist with your left hand. This action causes no injury or pain to the person. It is simply to hold the person's right arm so that it doesn't move.

3 Forcefully, snap the flashlight upward so that its head area impacts against the person's arm slightly above the elbow. This action should break the person's elbow. Use appropriate follow-up measures.

NOTE: Although the person has just tried to kill you, you still have a duty to help the person. Hence, administer whatever medical treatment is necessary and/or transport the person to the hospital.

SITUATION: You are being choked from the front by a person who has grasped you around the neck and the throat with both hands.

ACTION:

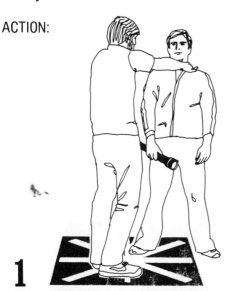

1

A person chokes you from the front by placing his/her hands around your throat and neck. Notice that you are not standing directly in front of the person.

2

Quickly, move the flashlight across your body by bending your right elbow. Grasp the flashlight behind its head with your left hand--palm down. The reason to properly position yourself and the flashlight and to properly use a defensive escape technique.

3

Release the barrel of the flashlight with your right hand. Regrip it by grasping the tail cap portion of the flashlight--palm up.

4

Forcefully, pull your right hand toward your stomach. Allowing the barrel of the flashlight to pivot between your left thumb and index finger, push the head of the flashlight into the person's lower abdominal or groin area. This action should make the person release the grip around your neck. Use appropriate follow-up measures.

SITUATION: You are being choked from the front by a person who has grasped you around the neck and the throat with both of his/her hands.

ACTION:

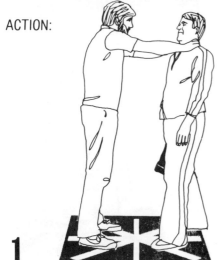

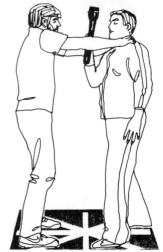

1 A person begins to choke you from the front by placing his/her hands around your throat and neck.

2 Holding the flashlight in your right hand, quickly insert it between the person's arms by bending your right arm at the elbow. **NOTE:** It doesn't matter which end of the flashlight is pointing upward.

3 After inserting the flashlight between the person's arms, place the barrel of the flashlight over the person's right radial (top wrist) bone. Place the barrel of the flashlight as close to the person's wrist as possible. The reason: the wrist bone is closer to the skin surface where the wrist and the hand join, making easier application of the technique.

4 Quickly grasp the barrel of the flashlight with your left hand. Simultaneously, place both of your thumbs under the person's wrist, keeping them in front of the flashlight. The web of your hands (the skin between your thumbs and index fingers) must be held tightly against each side of the person's right wrist. The reason: to keep the flashlight stable.

5

Forcefully squeeze the flashlight against the person's radial (top wrist) bone, while slightly rotating the flashlight toward the person's elbow. This movement should create pain, making the person's knees bend, while simultaneously removing his/her right hand from your neck. Remember to maintain pressure on the person's wrist for pain compliance.

6

Force the person onto the ground--on his/her back--by squeezing the flashlight very tightly on the right wrist and by rotating it toward the person's right elbow. Simultaneously, make a quarter turn by stepping backward with your left foot. This should cause the person to lie on his/her back.

7

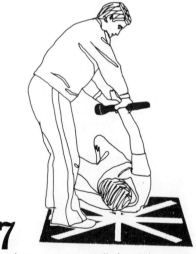

Keeping pressure applied to the person's wrist with the flashlight, pull his/her arm upward and begin to walk around the person's head.

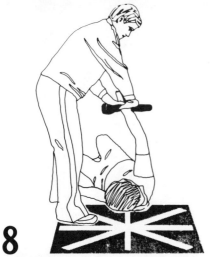

8

To roll the person onto his/her stomach, quickly walk around the person's head. As you walk, keep the person's arm straight which will make it easier to roll him/her over.

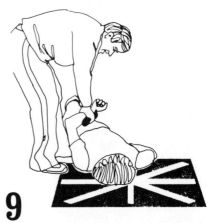

9

After the person is on his/her stomach, fold the person's right arm at the elbow, and kneel on the person.

SITUATION: You are being choked from behind by a person who has grasped you around the neck and throat areas with his/her forearm.

ACTION:

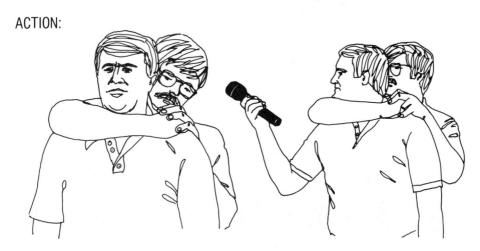

1

A person chokes you from behind by placing his/her forearm across your throat.

2

Immediately, turn your head and throat into the "V" (crook of the arm) of the attacker's arm. The reason: so that you can breath. Simultaneously, raise the hand which is holding the flashlight by bending it at the elbow.

3

Place the edge of the tail cap portion of the flashlight against the center of the person's forearm. Also, grasp the barrel of the flashlight with your free hand.

4

With the edge of the tail cap positioned in the center of the person's forearm, forcefully press the flashlight into the person's forearm muscles and tendons using both of your hands. Keep firm pressure on this area until the attacker begins to release his/her grip.

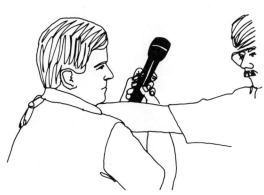

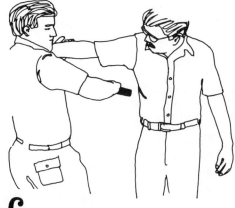

5

As the person releases his/her grip, step toward the elbow that is around your neck. This action should place you beside the attacker, and should also straighten his/her arm. **NOTE:** As you step, keep pressure on the person's forearm muscles and tendons.

6

After you're beside the person, forcefully push the tail cap of the flashlight into the attacker's rib cage area. This action should break or crack the person's ribs. Use appropriate follow-up measures.

SITUATION: An attacker, who is sitting upon your stomach, chokes you around the throat with both of his/her hands.

ACTION:

1

After a short scuffle, an attacker has you pinned on your back. (S)He is sitting upon your stomach and choking you around the throat with both of his/her hands. **NOTE:** Your holding the flashlight in your right hand.

2

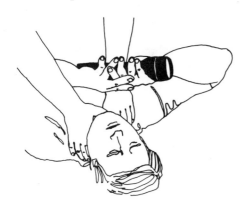

Quickly, place the barrel of the flashlight over the person's wrist. Since you're holding the flashlight in your right hand, you will most likely apply it to his/her left wrist. The reason: it's the closest wrist to your right hand.

Place the barrel over the person's radial (top wrist) bone. Simultaneously, place both of your thumbs under the person's wrist. The web of your hands (the skin between your thumbs and index fingers) must be held tightly against each side of the person's left wrist. The reason: to keep the flashlight stable.

3

Squeeze the barrel tightly against the person's wrist, while rolling the barrel slightly toward the person's elbow. This action should cause the person's hand to release its grip. Continue squeezing the barrel until the person rolls off your stomach and to your right. Use appropriate follow-up measures.

Chapter XI

SELF-DEFENSE:
DEFENSIVE FLASHLIGHT TECHNIQUES

This section's focus is upon defensive flashlight escape techniques which you can use should the violator grab you or place you into a bearhug or a full nelson. While there are many defensive techniques which could be shown and used, the ones that were selected should work for most everyone. Therefore, practice them.

SITUATION: A person grabs you by the left wrist using his/her left hand.

ACTION:

1
Standing in the interrogation position--firearm away from the person--and holding the flashlight by its barrel at shoulder height, you begin talking to the person. Suddenly, (s)he grabs your left wrist with his/her left hand.

2
Immediately, rotate your left arm to the left so that the top of the person's left hand is facing you. Also, begin to lower the head of the flashlight toward the top of the person's hand by bending your right arm at the elbow.

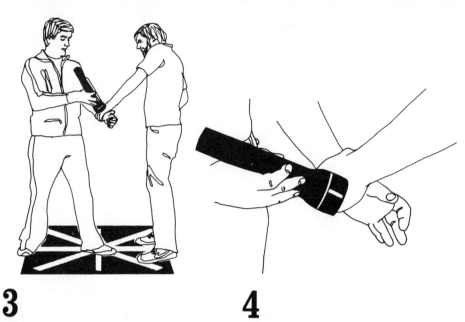

3

While keeping the flashlight on an angle so the person cannot easily grab the barrel, place the edge of the flashlight head against the top of the person's left hand.

4

A close-up view showing the proper position of how the flashlight head is pushed against the top of the person's hand.

5

Forcefully, press the edge of the flashlight head into the top of the person's left hand. Simultaneously, step backward with your left leg. The reasons: to unbalance the person by pulling him/her forward; to keep your balance; and to extend the person's arm which reduces the strength in his/her left forearm. Use appropriate follow-up measures.

NOTE: This defensive technique will also work using the edge of the tail cap. If your flashlight has a sharp edge around its head, which would cut the person's hand, then use the edge of the tail cap. The reason: to avoid cutting the person's hand.

SITUATION: While talking to a person, (s)he grabs your wrist with one hand and attempts to punch you in the face with the other hand.

ACTION:

1

During the conversation, the person suddenly grabs your left wrist with his/her right hand.

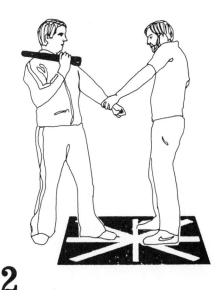

2

After grasping your left wrist, the person raises his/her right hand in preparation to punch you in the face.

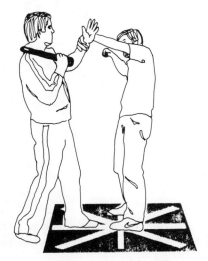

3

Keeping your left hand open, rotate your hand and wrist in a small semi-circular counterclockwise motion.

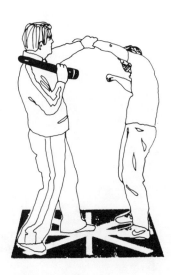

4

Continue the motion until you can grasp his/her left wrist with your left hand.

5

Pull the person's wrist downward until his/her arm is straightened. Next, snap the flashlight forward in a downward arc so that the barrel strikes the person's tricep area. Use appropriate follow-up measures. **NOTE:** This action may break the person's elbow.

SITUATION: From behind, a person grabs you around the waist pinning your arms to your sides.

ACTION:

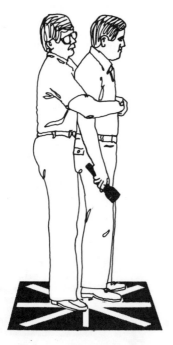

1

From behind, a person grabs you around the waist pinning your arms to your side.

2

Holding the flashlight by its barrel in your strong hand, lift your arm to waist height by bending your right elbow.

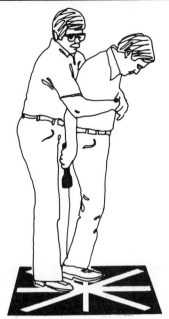

3

Forcefully thrust your arm downward in the direction of the person's lower abdominal area.

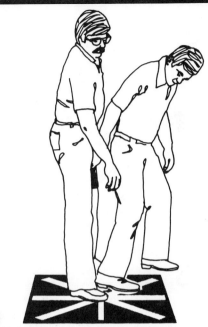

4

Having forcefully pushed the head of the flashlight into the person's lower abdominal area, (s)he should release your arms. Use appropriate follow-up measures.

SITUATION: From behind, a person grabs you around the waist pinning your arms to your sides.

ACTION:

1

From behind, a person grabs you around the waist pinning your arms to your side.

2

Holding the flashlight by its barrel in your strong hand, lift your arm to waist height by bending your right elbow.

3

Quickly, raise the arm holding the flashlight by bending at the elbow. The palm of the hand which is holding the flashlight should be up for ease in application of the technique.

4

With your free hand, grasp the flashlight barrel and your other hand. Using both of your hands, forcefully push the edge of the tail into the top of the person's hand. Keep the pressure until you feel the person's hands loosen.

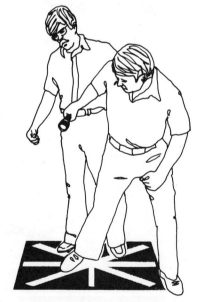

5

As you feel the person's hands loosen, take a step forward with your weak leg. Also, bend your right arm at the elbow so that the flashlight is waist high. The reason: to prepare for a follow-up technique, if necessary.

6

Only if necessary, forcefully push the tail cap of the flashlight into the person's lower abdominal area. **NOTE:** DO NOT strike the person in the solar plexus area. The reason: death or serious injury may result. Use appropriate follow-up measures.

7

You may also use another defensive flashlight technique, as a follow-up or, if necessary, as a second part of -5. Bending your right arm at the elbow so that the flashlight is waist high, forcefully snap your right wrist downward. Simultaneously, move your arm in a downward arc so that the head of the flashlight impacts into the person's lower abdominal or groin area. Use appropriate follow-up measures.

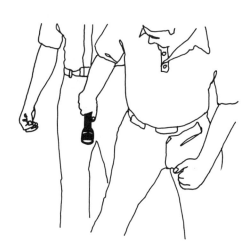

SITUATION: A person applies a full nelson hold on you.

ACTION:

1

A person applies a full nelson hold on you.

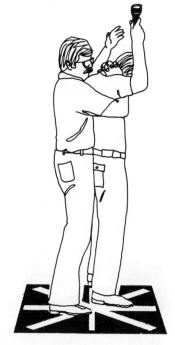

2

Immediately lift both of your arms over your head.

3

Holding the flashlight with both of your hands, forcefully push the tail cap into the top of the attacker's hands or fingers.

4

As the person's hands and arms release the grip on your neck, step forward with your weak foot. Lift the flashlight so that it is about shoulder height, by bending your right arm at the elbow.

5

As you feel the person's hands loosen, take a step forward with your weak leg. Also, bend your right arm at the elbow so that the flashlight is waist high. The reason: to prepare for a follow-up technique, if necessary.

6

Only if necessary, forcefully push the tail cap of the flashlight into the person's lower abdominal area. **NOTE:** DO NOT strike the person in the solar plexus area. The reason: death or serious injury may result. Use appropriate follow-up measures.

Chapter XII

VEHICLE EXTRACTIONS:
DEFENSIVE FLASHLIGHT TECHNIQUES

This section's focus is upon the safe and the effective removal of a driver who refuses to exit his/her vehicle after you tell them to get out. The defensive techniques which are presented in this section are designed to work on the basis of pain compliance. If the driver is extremely intoxicated or on drugs, these techniques may not work as well as intended.

SITUATION: A motorist refuses to exit the vehicle after you tell him/her to come out.

ACTION:

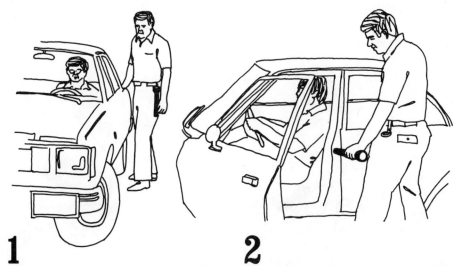

1

Approach the vehicle and the driver in a safely prescribed manner.

2

After the driver refuses to exit the vehicle, open the driver's door. Next remove your flashlight and hold it in your left hand. For ease in technique application, grasp the barrel of the flashlight--police-style--just behind its head. Point the tail cap toward the driver's wrist. **NOTE:** You may hold the flashlight in either hand. It is recommended, however, that you hold it in your non-gun hand. The reason: to aid in the drawing of your firearm.

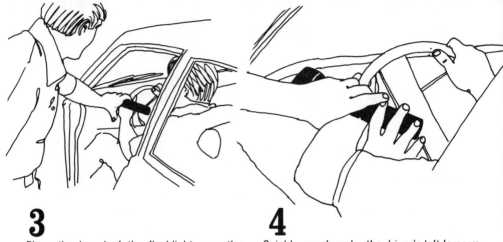

3

Place the barrel of the flashlight over the driver's left radial (top wrist) bone. The tail cap should be pointing toward the passenger's door. Notice that your left thumb is pointing downward.

4

Quickly, reach under the driver's left forearm with your right hand and grasp the barrel of the flashlight with your fingers. Simultaneously, place both of your thumbs under the person's wrist. The web of your hands (the skin between your thumbs and index fingers) must be held tightly against each side of the person's left wrist. The reason: to keep the flashlight stable.

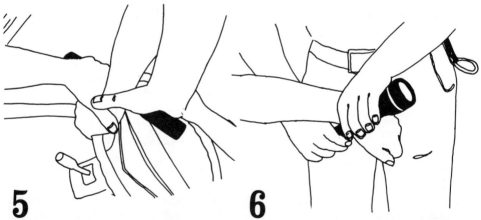

5

View looking upward showing the proper placement of the thumbs and the flashlight. After your thumbs are properly positioned, forcefully lift your right forearm. This action should lift the driver's left forearm upward forming a "block", should (s)he decide to punch you with his/her right hand. Simultaneously, squeeze the flashlight against the driver's wrist.

6

Having tightly squeezed the barrel against the driver's left wrist, slightly rotate the barrel toward the driver's thumb while forcefully pulling the flashlight toward your waist. This action should remove the driver's left hand from the steering wheel. For maximum pain compliance, keep pressure upon the driver's wrist by squeezing the barrel.

7

As you pull the flashlight toward you, step back with your left foot. This action will help you to remove the driver from the vehicle. After the driver is placed upon the ground, you may handcuff him/her, or you may use other appropriate follow-up measures.

8

If traffic or debris will not permit you to place the driver in a prone position, you may walk him/her to the left rear quarter of the vehicle. Now, handcuff him/her or use other appropriate follow-up measures.

SITUATION: A motorist refuses to exit the vehicle after you tell him/her to come out.

ACTION:

1

Approach the vehicle in a safely prescribed manner.

NOTE: You may hold the flashlight in either hand. However, it is recommended that you hold it in your non-gun hand. The reason: to aid in the drawing of your firearm.

2

After the driver refuses to exit the vehicle, remove your flashlight and hold it in your left hand. For ease in technique application, grasp the barrel of the flashlight--police-style--just behind its head. Staying to the rear of the driver's door jamb for safety reasons (you reduce the chances of being pushed into traffic should (s)he thrust open the door), begin to insert the barrel of the flashlight through the open driver's window.

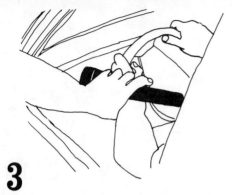

3

Place the barrel of the flashlight over the driver's left radial (top wrist) bone. The tail cap should be pointing toward the passenger's door. Notice that your left thumb is pointing downward.

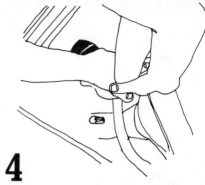

4

Quickly, insert your right arm through the open driver's window. Reach under the driver's left forearm with your right hand and grasp the barrel of the flashlight with your fingers. Simultaneously, place both of your thumbs under the driver's wrist. The web of your hands (the skin between your thumbs and index fingers) must be held tightly against each side of the driver's left wrist. The reason: to keep the flashlight stable.

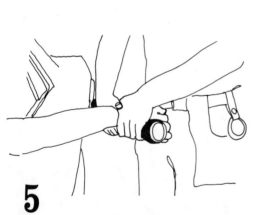

5

After your thumbs are properly positioned, forcefully lift your right forearm. This action should lift the driver's left forearm upward forming a "block", should (s)he decide to punch you with his/her right hand. Simultaneously, squeeze the flashlight against the driver's wrist pulling the flashlight toward you through the open driver's window. This action should remove the driver's left hand from the steering wheel. For maximum pain compliance, keep pressure upon the driver's wrist by squeezing the barrel.

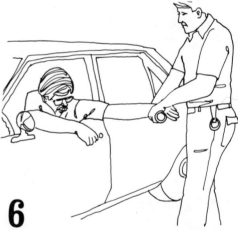

6

Staying behind the driver's door, pull his/her arm through the open window. Next, advise the driver to open the door by grasping the outside door handle. Make sure that you watch the driver's right hand. The reason: There have been situations where a driver had glued a holster with a handgun beneath the driver's window. Hence, when (s)he appeared to be opening the door from the inside, (s)he was really removing the firearm.

7

Tell the driver to push open the door. As (s)he does move to your left. Position the driver as shown while keeping pressure on his/her left wrist.

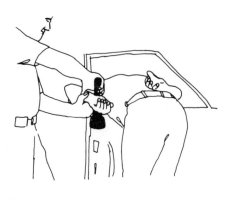

8

After the driver is positioned through the open window, ask him/her to put his/her right hand on the small of the back. After the right hand is in place, take a step toward the person while simultaneously bending the driver's left arm.

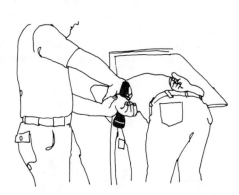

9

There is a possibility that the driver will begin to fight you at this point. Although the reasons for the resistance may never be known, you must remain alert for danger during the removal of the driver. Should (s)he begin to struggle prepare to "knee" the person in the thigh.

10

When the driver begins to fight, bend your right leg at the knee. Lifting your right foot off the ground, forcefully strike the driver's thigh area with your right knee. Your focus should be on the driver's trouser seam, about three inches above the knee joint. This action should result in the cramping of the driver's leg. The result: (s)he should stop resisting, thus allowing you to complete the technique.

11

Whether or not the driver resists you, after bending his/her left arm, remove the flashlight and grasp his/her right thumb.

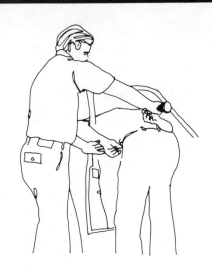

12

A close-up view showing how to properly grasp the driver's thumb. To grasp the thumb, simply place the barrel of the flashlight on the thumbnail side of the thumb. Your thumb should be on the thumb print side of the driver's thumb. For maximum pain compliance, squeeze the flashlight barrel against the thumb bone. CAUTION: **DO NOT** bend the driver's thumb. The reason: it may break.

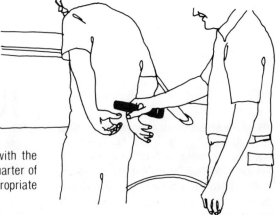

13

Having grasped the driver's thumb with the barrel, lead him/her to the left rear quarter of the car for handcuffing or other appropriate follow-up measures.

SITUATION: A motorist refuses to exit the vehicle after you tell him/her to come out.

ACTION:

1

Approach the vehicle in a safely prescribed manner.

After the driver refuses to exit the vehicle, open the driver's door. Next, remove your flashlight and hold it in your left hand. For ease in technique application, grasp the barrel of the flashlight--police-style--just behind its head. Point the tail cap toward the driver's wrist. Notice that both of the driver's hands are gripping the steering wheel at the base of the wheel. **NOTE:** You may hold the flashlight in either hand. It is recommended however, that you hold it in your non-gun hand. The reason: to aid in the drawing of your firearm.

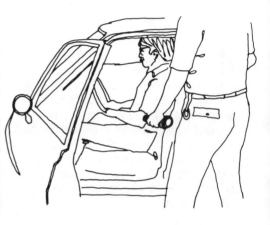

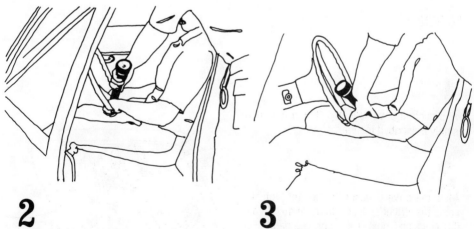

2

Press the edge of the tail cap against the top of the driver's left hand. This action should cause pain and also cause the driver to loosen his/her grip on the steering wheel.

3

Having pressed the tail cap against the driver's left hand, remove it from the driver's hand and quickly place the barrel over the driver's left wrist. Place the barrel over the driver's left radial (top wrist) bone. The tail cap should be pointing toward the passenger's door. Notice that your left thumb is pointing downward.

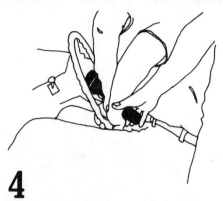

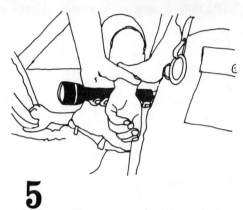

4

Quickly, reach under the driver's left forearm with your right hand, and grasp the barrel of the flashlight with your fingers. Simultaneously, place both of your thumbs under the person's wrist. The web of your hands (the skin between your thumbs and index fingers) must be held tightly against each side of the person's left wrist. The reason: to keep the flashlight stable.

5

Having tightly squeezed the barrel against the driver's left wrist, slightly rotate the barrel toward the driver's thumb while forcefully pulling the flashlight toward your waist. This action should remove the driver's left hand from the steering wheel.

SITUATION: A motorist refuses to exit the vehicle after you tell him/her to come out.

ACTION:

1

Approach the vehicle and the driver in a safely prescribed manner.

2

After the driver refuses to exit the vehicle, open the driver's door. Next, remove your flashlight and hold it in your left hand. For ease in technique application, grasp the barrel of the flashlight near the tail cap. Point the tail cap toward the driver. **NOTE:** You may hold the flashlight in either hand. It is recommended however, that you hold it in your non-gun hand. The reason: to aid in the drawing of your firearm.

3

Pinch the driver's ear between the edge of the tail cap and your left thumb. This "clothes-pin" type technique should be very effective in "helping" the driver exit the vehicle.

4

A close-up view showing the pinching of the driver's ear. Simply place the edge of the tail cap against the outside of the ear; place your left thumb behind the ear. For pain compliance, pinch the ear. Use appropriate follow-up procedures.

Chapter XIII

KNIVES:
DEFENSIVE FLASHLIGHT TECHNIQUES

When the violator pulls a knife, draw your weapon. FAST!! A knife is nothing to play with, even if you're a skilled martial artist. Unless you incapacitate the violator to a point where (s)he can't attack you, be prepared to get cut.

There may be situations, however, when you can't draw your weapon. For example, the violator takes you by surprise or you're being confronted and challenged in the middle of a busy shopping mall. Coupled with these situations is the need for you to react safely and quickly. Therefore, practice these techniques with a little more zest and seriousness.

SITUATION: A person who is holding a knife in the right hand threatens to stab you.

ACTION:

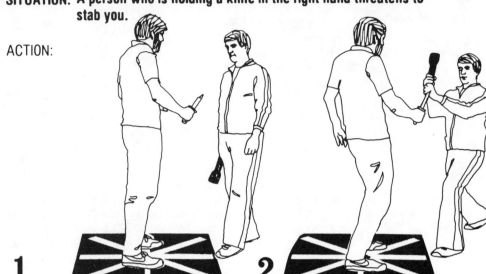

1
A person who is holding a knife in the right hand threatens to stab you. You are holding the flashlight in your right hand having grasped it by the barrel so that its head is pointing downward.

2
Quickly, raise the flashlight by bending your right arm at the elbow so that its head is pointing upward. Simultaneously, grasp the tail cap section of the barrel with your left hand, while stepping backward and to the right with your right foot. Stepping to the right should do the following: move you from the line of attack, and move you so that you can better see the person's wrist.

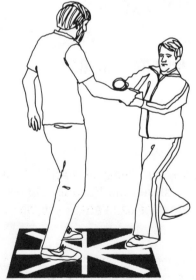

3
Forcefully, snap the flashlight in a downward arc so that its head or barrel strikes the person's right wrist or forearm area. For more striking power when you snap the flashlight downward, forcefully pull up on the tail cap portion with your left hand.

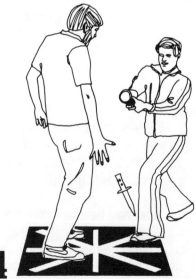

4
This action should break the person's right wrist or forearm causing him/her to drop the knife. Use appropriate follow-up measures.

SITUATION: a person, holding a knife in the right hand attempts to stab you in the stomach.

ACTION:

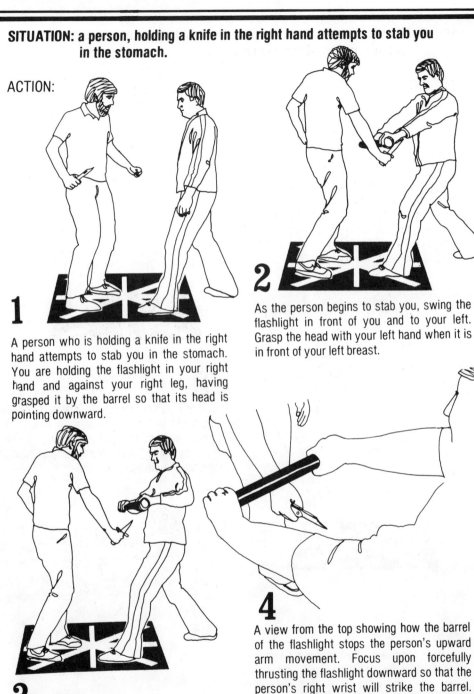

1

A person who is holding a knife in the right hand attempts to stab you in the stomach. You are holding the flashlight in your right hand and against your right leg, having grasped it by the barrel so that its head is pointing downward.

2

As the person begins to stab you, swing the flashlight in front of you and to your left. Grasp the head with your left hand when it is in front of your left breast.

3

Using both of your arms, forcefully thrust the horizontally-held flashlight downward, away from you and toward the person's right wrist. The reasons: to block and to "stuff" the attack.

4

A view from the top showing how the barrel of the flashlight stops the person's upward arm movement. Focus upon forcefully thrusting the flashlight downward so that the person's right wrist will strike the barrel. This action should do the following: break person's right wrist causing him/her to drop the knife; and/or stop the person's upward motion before much speed and thus power is generated. Use appropriate follow-up measures.

SITUATION: A person, holding a knife in the right hand attempts to cut you a horizontal slashling motion.

ACTION:

1

A person who is holding a knife in the right hand attempts to cut you using a horizontal slashing motion. You are holding the flashlight in your right hand and against your right leg, having grasped it by the barrel so that its head is pointing downward.

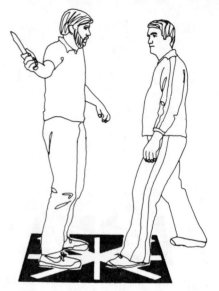

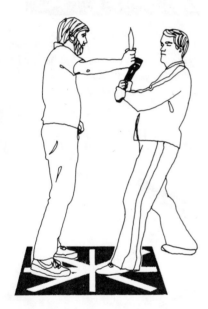

2

As the person begins to slash, raise the flashlight by bending your right arm at the elbow so that its head is pointing upward. Simultaneously, grasp the tail cap section of the barrel with your left hand.

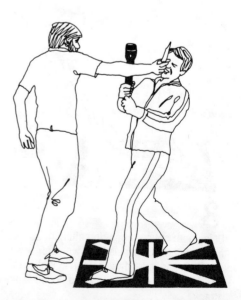

3

Forcefully, snap the flashlight in a downward arc so that its head or barrel strikes the person's right wrist or forearm area. For more striking power when you snap the flashlight downward, push the tail cap portion of the barrel to the right using your left hand.

SITUATION: A person attempts to stab you with a knife in an over-the-head manner.

ACTION:

1

A person who is holding a knife in the right hand raises his/her right arm in preparation to stab you. **NOTE:** Your are holding the flashlight against your right leg by grasping the tail cap portion of its barrel with your right hand.

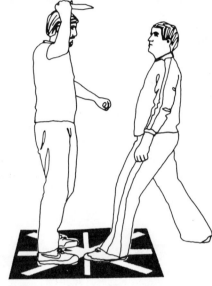

2

As the person raises his/her right arm, swing the flashlight in front of you and to your left. Grasp the head with your left hand when it is in front of your left shoulder. Next, using both of your arms, forcefully thrust the horizontally-held flashlight upward, away from you and toward the person's right wrist. The reasons: To block and to "stuff" the attack.

3

Focus upon forcefully thrusting the flashlight upward so that the person's right wrist will strike the barrel. This action should do the following: break the person's right wrist causing him/her to drop the knife; and/or stop the person's downward motion before much speed and thus power is generated. To help you block the person's downward motion, step into the attack using your left leg.

NOTE: If possible, keep the horizontally-held flashlight in front of and above your head. The reason: to reduce the possibility of the knife blade striking your head or facial area after you have effectively blocked the attack. Remember, as you step in to block the attack, keep your left leg slightly bent at the knee and keep both of your arms fully extended in front of you at a 45⁰ angle.

4

As soon as you have blocked the attack, parry the person's wrist and forearm downward and to your right. The reason: to move the knife away from you, and to unbalance the person. This can be done by pushing on the head of the flashlight with your left hand, while turning slightly at the waist. You can also pull the tail cap portion of the flashlight which is in your right hand toward your face by slightly bending your right elbow.

5

Keeping your left forearm against the person's right arm, release the head of the flashlight with your left hand. Raise the flashlight so that its head is pointing upward and its tail cap is pointing downward. The reason: to prepare for, if necessary, a follow-up strike to the person's right forearm and/or wrist.

6

Keeping your left forearm against the person's right arm so (s)he can't move it to stab you, forcefully snap your right wrist downward so that the head or barrel of the flashlight hits the person's right wrist or forearm area. This action should break the person's right wrist or forearm, causing him/her to drop the knife. Use appropriate follow-up measures.

Chapter XIV

WEAPON RETENTION:
DEFENSIVE FLASHLIGHT TECHNIQUES

Since one of every five police officers (20%) is shot with his/her own firearm, this chapter is extremely important. Retaining your weapon is vital to your well-being and/or to the safety of others who may be nearby. And remember, every time you're on a call, there's a weapon present--YOURS.

A special note of thanks goes to weapon retention pioneer, James W. Lindell, who kindly reviewed the contents or this chapter.

SITUATION: While talking to a person, (s)he reaches for your weapon, in an attempt to draw it upside down.

ACTION:

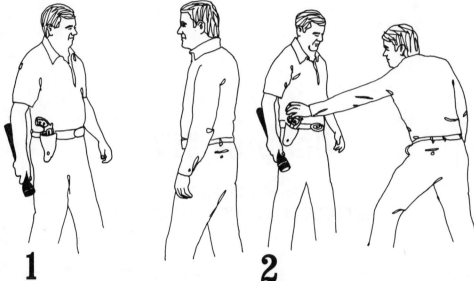

1

Standing in the interrogation position (firearm away from the person) and holding the flashlight civilian-style, you begin talking to the person.

2

Suddenly, the person reaches for your weapon with a left hand, placing his/her finger on the trigger.

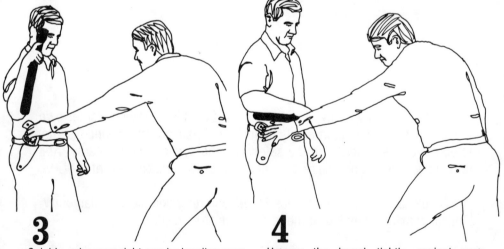

3

Quickly, raise your right arm by bending your right elbow.

NOTE: There is a possibility that the person's left wrist may be broken upon its coming into contact with the flashlight.

4

Holding the barrel tightly against your forearm, forcefully thrust your arm downward. this action should cause the barrel of the flashlight to strike the person's left wrist or forearm. Use appropriate follow-up measures.

SITUATION: While talking to a person, another individual approaches from the rear and attempts to take your weapon.

ACTION:

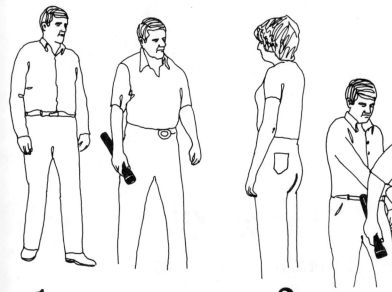

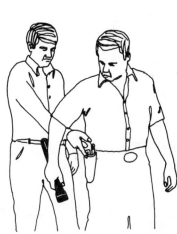

1

Standing in the interrogation position (firearm away form the person) and holding the flashlight civilian-style, you begin talking to a person. From behind, another individual approaches.

2

Before you are aware of the second person, (s)he reaches for your weapon with his/her right hand.

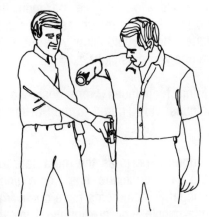

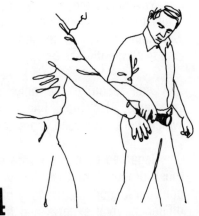

3

Quickly, raise your right arm by bending your right elbow.

4

Holding the barrel tightly against your forearm, forcefully thrust your arm downward. This action should cause the barrel of the flashlight to strike the person's right wrist or forearm.

5
Only if necessary, forcefully push the tail cap portion of the barrel into the person's stomach or lower abdominal area. After striking the violator's wrist, pivot your body so that your weapon is removed from his/her reach. Use appropriate follow-up measures.
NOTE: Do not push the tail cap portion of the barrel into the person's solar plexus area. The reason: it may cause serious injury or death.

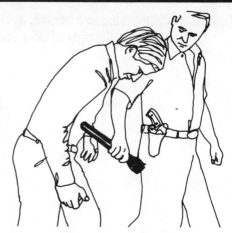

Chapter XV

FLASHLIGHTS AND FIREARMS

Night firing with a weapon and with a flashlight has always been a marriage out of necessity. You had to have enough light to see the room, the building or an intruder, yet not too much light or (s)he may see you. If (s)he saw you first, then your life may be in the other's hands, especially if (s)he were armed.

You also need a technique which would allow you the maximum flexibility to shoot, to seek cover, to move about and to maximize your safety. Simultaneously, you needed a technique which would allow you to quickly and to efficiently use both your firearm and your flashlight.*

Until recently, the only night firing techniques were designed for handguns. Also, these handgun techniques were limited to the FBI tactics which were developed years ago.

Regarded by many police and handgun experts as the most safe and most practical method for years, the FBI techinque has come under considerable criticism. Many of these negative comments have come from officer survival experts and from those people who are involved in "the new combat pistolcraft". Before their critical views are presented and discussed, let's first discuss and show the FBI night firing technique.

The **FBI Night Firing Technique** can be described as follows:

- The principle behind the FBI flashlight is to delude an opponent as to the officer's exact position.[1]

- To properly perform this technique you: hold your handgun in your strong hand; hold the flashlight in your weak hand; and hold the flashlight in front of your body and at arm's length. (At approximately a 45° angle forward and out to the side).

- The **advantages** of this technique are: it's simple to use; it doesn't take a lot of training; it has a good track record in the field as having worked successfully in non-combative situations; and it is a good technique when you desire to scan the scene for possible danger.

- The **disadvantages** of this techinque are: it is often improperly used resulting in the officer's illumination of his/her own body; it can develop a sense of "false security" in the person using it if the shortcomings are not presented; it forces the officer to hold the flashlight in an unnatural position; it fails to give an officer the needed flexibility to turn and suddenly spotlight a target that may be behind him; and it reduces the officer's overall flexibility to respond to a changing environment.

To "correct" the shortcomings of the FBI technique, many firearms experts have developed many new and equally controversial night firing techniques. As you read the following descriptions of the various techniques and then view each of the techniques, keep an open mind. This request is being made because some of the techniques are sure to draw your criticism.

Your criticism will probably focus upon where to properly and to safely hold the flashlight. As Massad Ayoob, noted firearms expert says, "This brings us to an argument that will probably never be resolved: is it better to tumble for a second with a light out at your side trying to find your target but also hopefully luring his own gunsights away from your body? Or is it better to use a direct point that illuminates the subject immediately so you can identify him as friend or foe, shoot him squarely if you have to, and hope that you do it before he shoots at the light?[2] With Ayoob's questions in mind, let's continue.

*A ten-year study involving more than 6,000 firearm incidents was conducted by the New York City Police Department. Among the findings, the report cited that flashlights were used in the initial search and as a baton. No incidents were reported where flashlights were used to spot targets during actual shootings.

One of the primary reasons for the development of the following handgun night firing techniques is to use a straight point of light. These techniques use a two-handed format and emphasize a straight point of light. According to Ayoob and others who are regarded as experts in combat pistolcraft, a straight point is better for more speed and precision.

In essence, these techniqes bring your hands together. This will allow you: to better control the flashlight; to better control the handgun; to behave more reactively when you confront danger; to react as a team-- flashlight, handgun and eyes all pointing and looking in the same direction and operating as one unit; and to reduce reaction time both in preparation for response and in actual response time.

The Ayoob Method

This technique was developed by Massad Ayoob. The Ayoob night firing technique can be described as follows:

- The principle behind the Ayoob method appears to be the fast identification of another person as friend or foe and to simultaneously blind him/her with the flashlight beam.

- To properly perform this technique you: hold your handgun in your strong hand; hold the flashlight--civilian-style--in your weak hand; bring both hands together at eye level; push both hands outward by extending your arms in a very fluid motion; and press the bases of the thumbs together.

- The apparent **advantages** of the Ayoob method are: it centers both the flashlight beam and the gunsights on the opponent; it naturally positions the beam upward and into the opponent's eyes which should temporarily blind him/her; it works best when firing from eye-level; it gives you excellent recoil control of the flashlight; and it gives you maximum speed and good accuracy in poor light and at unfavorable angles.

- The **disadvantages** of the Ayoob method are: it's held in front of your body; it doesn't work well in a low-hold position; and if the opponent shoots first and aims at the lightbeam, you could be shot in the head or in the upper body area.

The Chapman Method

This technique was developed by Ray Chapman. The Chapman night firing technique can be described as follows:

- The apparent principle behind the Chapman method appears to be the fast identification of an opponent as friend or foe and to simultaneously illuminate the target.

- To properly perform this technique you: hold your handgun in your strong hand; hold the flashlight--civilian-style--in your weak hand; bring both hands together at eye level; push both hands outward by extending your arms in a very fluid motion; and encircle the shooting hand with the fingers of your weak hand.

- The apparent **advantages** of the Chapman method are: it centers both the flashlight beam and the gunsights on the opponent; it works best when firing from eye level; it gives you good accuracy, especially at a long distance; and it gives you maximum speed and good accuracy in poor light and at unfavorable angles.

- The apparent **disadvantages** of the Chapman method are: it's held in front of your body; it doesn't work well in a low-hold position; it's awkward for those people with small hands (your fingers can't cup the shooting hand); and if the opponent shoots first and aims at the light beam, you could be shot in the head or the upper body area.

The Cirillo Method

This technique was reportedly developed by Jim Cirillo, an ex-New York Police officer. In some circles this method is called the New York technique. The Cirillo technique can be described as follows:

- The principle behind the Cirillo method appears to be the fast identification of an opponent as friend or foe, while simultaneously illuminating the target.

- To properly perform this technique you, hold your handgun in your strong hand; hood the flashlight--civilian-style--in your weak hand; bring both hands together at stomach level so that your weak hand is under your strong hand; and you keep both of your elbows slightly bent and positioned at your rib cage.

- The apparent **advantages** of the Cirillo method are: it works especially well with C-cell flashlights; it centers both the flashlight beam and the firearm on the opponent; it places the light beam in a position to illuminate the upper body of the opponent; and it gives you excellent coordination of both the light beam and the barrel of the handgun (your weak hand fingertips can be used to cup your shooting hand).

- The apparent **disadvantages** of the Cirillo method are: it's held in front of your body; it doesn't work well in a high-hold position; it doesn't give you good control of the weapon (it's as if firing one-handed and, depending upon the type of handgun, shots can go vertically low or high); you can easily move the handgun upward when you place your weak hand under your strong hand; and if the opponent shoots first and aims at the light beam, you could be shot in the mid-section of your body.

The Harries Method

This technique was developed by Mike Harries. The Harries night firing technique can be described as follows:

- The principle behind the Harries technique appears to be the fast identification of an opponent as friend or foe, while simultaneously illuminating the target.

- To properly perform this technique you: hold your handgun in your strong hand; hold the flashlight--civilian-style--in your weak hand; place your weak hand on the barrel of the flashlight, directly behind its head; place your weak arm under your strong arm; place the top of your hands together; press the top of your hands together firmly; extend the handgun to eye level; and keep both of your arms slightly bent at the elbows.

- The apparent **advantages** of the Harries method are: it rests the strong hand on the weak wrist, hence a possibility of improved accuracy; it "locks" the tops of the hands together because the hands are pressed together (again, this might improve your accuracy); it focuses the flashlight where the handgun is pointed; and it gives you better control of the weapon than does a one-hand hold.

- The apparent **disadvantages** of the Harries method are: it's held in front of your body; it's more difficult to learn than the other techniques; it's not an easy position to get into when you need speed and accuracy (crossing the wrists takes time); it reduces your ability to react to the threats from behind and at your sides; it doesn't work well with multi-cell flashlights (they're too long); and if the opponent shoots first and aims at the beam, you could be shot in the head area.

Regarding these handgun techniques, practice all of them. Unless you do, you will not know which one will work the best for you. Possibly, more than one will work for you. Fine. Select those techniques which are comfortable for you, which are going to give you the flexibility to safely and to quickly respond to a threatening situation and which are going to give you the advantage over the opponent.

Lastly, do not totally discard the FBI technique. Its strength is in the scanning of dark and dangerous areas. And remember, many times it's not the technique which is at fault, but rather the way it is applied to the situation.

Long-Gun

Using a flashlight and a long-barreled weapon has always posed a problem. For example, if you needed both hands to hold the weapon, you couldn't hold the flashlight, too. Fortunately, some people in the firearms field were creative and devised a technique whereby you can hold both the weapon and the flashlight.

Although the person who developed this technique is unknown to the author, the following technique was shown to him by Dennis Anderson of Calibre Press, Inc. Dennis Anderson, with co-partner Charles Remsberg, are the creators of the highly-acclaimed **Street Survival® Seminars.** They are also co-publishers of the internationally-recognized **Bible** on survival tactics **STREET SURVIVAL: Tactics for Armed Encounters.**

It should be noted that neither Dennis Anderson nor Charles Remsberg developed the following technique. Rather, they have offered it to the police profession as a possible solution to the problem of holding a flashlight and shooting a long-barreled weapon. Since this technique doesn't have a name, the author will label it the belt technique.

The Belt Technique

This night firing technique can be described as follows:

- The principle behind the Belt Technique appears to be the stablizing of both the flashlight and the weapon as you offer cover for your partner during an arrest or field interrogation situation.

- To properly perform this technique you: hold the weapon in your strong hand; hold the flashlight--civilian-style--in your weak hand; "stuff" the tail cap portion of the barrel into your trousers at the waist band so that the head is pointing toward your weak side; turn on the flashlight with your weak hand; and aim the weapon at your opponent.

- The apparent **advantages** of the Belt technique are: it works with any cell size flashlight; it centers the flashlight beam on the opponent while you aim the weapon at him/her; it permits you to hold a light source and to hold a long-barreled weapon at the same time; it will, in most cases, place the light beam directly into the opponent's eyes causing temporary blindness; it will, in most cases, illuminate the upper portion of the opponent's body; it will allow you to change the direction of the light by simply rotating your hips; it minimizes your body exposure as you are only showing the opponent a side profile; and, if necessary, it could be used with a handgun, too.

- The apparent **disadvantages** of the Belt Technique are: it doesn't work too well with two-cell flashlights because there is not enough barrel length to stuff into your waist band; it doesn't work too well if you are wearing a three-quarter length jacket, a rain coat or a sport coat; if not executed properly, you can illuminate the barrel of your long weapon; and, if the opponent shoots first and aims at the light beam, you could be shot in the mid-to upper-body.

Regardless of the night firing technique you use, there are a few tips that you must remember. First, don't stand under a light source when you're using a night firing technique. The reason: the overhead light source will illuminate you. Hence, you will be a prime target for your opponent.

Second, don't stand in front of a light source (say 50 feet in front of a billboard or in front of a window where light is shining through). The reason: you will be silhouetted, again becoming an excellent target.

Lastly, try not to use a light source when you are dealing with an armed opponent. The reason: (s)he will be awaiting the opportunity to shoot at you the moment you turn on your flashlight.

To help you plan your strategy for encountering an unknown opponent, the next chapter, **Flashlight Survival Tactics** should give you some worthwhile lifesaving tips.

The FBI night firing technique. When used properly, there should be no spillover of light onto your body. If this occurs, you illuminate yourself and become a very visible target.

The so-called Cirillo night firing technique. Although comfortable to use, if the opponent shoots first, you will most likely be shot in the stomach or chest area.

The Harries night firing technique. Although it's difficult to learn, it gives you good control over the weapon because the top of your hands are pressed together. Again, if the opponent shoots first, you will most likely be shot in the chest or the head area.

The Chapman night firing technique. According to the experts, this method is better when your opponent is 10-15 yards away. If you have small hands you may find this technique awkward (your fingers can't encircle the shooting hand). Finally, if the opponent is armed and shoots first, you will most likely be shot in the face or the head area.

The Ayoob night firing technique. Of all the techniques, this is probably the easiest to use. When used properly, the flashlight beam will point upward and toward the opponent's eyes, temporarily blinding him/her. You shouldn't have to fumble with the light when using this technique.

The Ayoob method as seen from your viewpoint, when properly used, the light beam will shine in the opponent's eyes; the handgun is aimed at the midsection of the opponent. The experts claim that the Ayoob method is the better method when your opponent is less than 10 yards from you. Also, you can see your sights from the spillover of light from the flashlight. Should your opponent be armed and shoot first, you will most likely be shot in the chest or head area.

1

Belt Technique

Removing the flashlight from your ring with your weak hand--civilian-style--and then "stuffing" the tail cap portion of the barrel into your waist band area. As you insert the flashlight, hold the shotgun in your strong hand.

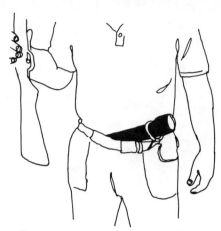

2

Close-up view showing the proper placement of the flashlight in your waist band area. As shown, you may wish to insert the flashlight without removing it from the ring. Some people have found that this method helps to stabilize the flashlight.

3

The view from the opponent's direction. Notice that the flashlight and the barrel of the weapon are pointing toward the opponent.

4

A view from the side showing the proper placement and the proper angle of the flashlight. When properly positioned, the flashlight beam should not illuminate the barrel of your weapon.

Chapter XVI

FLASHLIGHTS, TACTICS
AND YOUR SURVIVAL

Tactics.
Techniques
Survival
Death

Tactics, techniques, survival and death are all nouns. By themselves, each word is unrelated. For our purposes, however, each word becomes interrelated. The reasons: the use of poor **tactics** and/or **techniques,** the use of no **tactics** and/or **techniques** or the improper use of good **tactics** and/or **techniques** when confronted by an unknown and/or a potentially dangerous situation, will, most likely, reduce your chances of **survival** and possibly result in your **death** or the **death** of another person.

Tactics and techniques are the most important of these four words. Why? Because your survival and life, will, many times, be determined by the tactics you use or fail to use in a given situation. The objectives of this chapter are to first discuss, and second to show you a few of the widely-used and street-proven tactics and techniques which can be used with your flashlight. These tactics and techniques should help you to survive or help you to prevent a dangerous or a potentially dangerous situation from developing.

TACTICS

Tactics should be the first module in your survival system. Your tactics should consist of mental or written operational plans. The reason: the violator, many times, has an action plan to execute should (s)he need to use it. If you fail to have prepared an action plan, you'll be at both a tactical and a psychological disadvantage, should you need to confront the violator. (S)He will know how to go from situation A to situation B. Because you have failed to develop an action plan, should the situation suddenly change, you, most likely, will not know what to do.

If you work with another person, (s)he should know and should understand your tactics. When possible, the two of you should review, evaluate and up-date your plans. This type of participation should help to eliminate confusion when the two of you are called upon to use your action plan. Teamwork should be part of your tactical operations. Teamwork should help to eliminate confusion; it should help the team members work in concert to accomplish the same end result; and it should enhance every member's safety since each officer knows what and what not to do.

Included in your plans should be a "Don't" list. Knowing what not to do can sometimes have more positive outcomes than expected. Here are a few examples:

Don't enter a kill zone, should be near the top of your list. The kill zone is defined as the area the suspect can effectively control with hostile weapons fire.[1] This does not necessarily mean that your opponent must possess a firearm. It simply means, do not enter that area which **could** be controlled by a person who **might** be in possession of a firearm. Should the person have a firearm and you hastily enter the kill zone, you might be shot. And remember, in every situation where you're present there's a weapon--yours.

Don't be too overconfident should be on your list, too. The superman image should be fantasy thinking for you, not realistic thinking. Bullets will not bounce off your chest, knives will cut you and your bones can be broken if struck by a club, chair or fist. Therefore, use caution when approaching all situations.

Enough of the "Don't" list. Here are a few "Do's" that should be on your list for surviving.

Do stay alert. Don't get sloppy either mentally or physically. Pay attention to what's going on. Visually record your surroundings. Mentally record what's in your surroundings, what your opponent looks like; what your opponent is wearing; what your opponent says and does, and so forth. A relaxed mental state can get you hurt or even killed. Hence, stay alert.

Do develop a positive attitude. This is another important element of your positive mental conditioning. Keep a healthy attitude about your work and about the people with whom you come into contact. Most important, don't let overconfidence, the "I know it all" or "it won't happen to me" attitudes enter your mind.

Do stay physically fit. Be of sound mind and body. Your physical fitness may save your life or the lives of a partner or third party. For example, your heavy breathing, after climbing a flight of stairs, might be enough noise to "tell" an adversary your presence or your location. Hence, stay physically fit.

Do learn how to operate other types of flashlights. Learn how to operate as many types of flashlights as possible. Trying to learn how to turn on or off a flashlight in a dark hallway is not only dangerous, but also unnecessary. Learn how various flashlights operate. For example, because of the various types of switch assembly's, not all flashlights can be rolled across a floor. Learn the differences...your life may depend upon it.

Here are a few questions you should ask yourself after being given an unfamiliar flashlight.

- Is the flashlight made of plastic or of metal? (This fact is important should you be forced to block an attack by a person wielding a hard object such as a baseball bat.)
- Is the switch assembly push-button or slide-switch? (Knowing how to turn it off and on is important.)
- Will the flashlight roll smoothly across a flat surface? (as you will read and see later, this is an important tactical consideration.)
- Does the flashlight contain a spare bulb? (Should you need it, at least you know it's there.)
- Does the flashlight work? (It's better to discover that it doesn't work in the office than in a survival situation.)
- How are the bulb and the batteries changed? (If you are forced to change either of these items in the dark, at least you'll know how to do it.)

TECHNIQUES

After you have developed your tactical plans, you'll need good techniques to help carry out your plans. Techniques for our purposes are methods or procedures which you use in a given situation. For example, a wrist lock would be a technique available for use in the controlling of a violator.

Techniques can be labeled as preventive, positive, negative, defensive, offensive or survival oriented. The techniques which are discussed and shown below can possess all of these characteristics. For example, the flashing of the light beam directly into a person's eyes to temporarily blind him/her can be considered: preventive (you might be trying to stop him/her from moving forward); positive (you may gain a few more seconds to assess the person and/or the situation); negative (the suspect may not like it); defensive (your actions may be a defensive reaction to his/her agressive movements); offensive (you may have flashed the light beam into the person's eyes upon first contact with him/her so that you could gain a few seconds to assess the situation and assess with whom you are dealing); and, finally, survival oriented (you are looking after both his/her and your well-being).

Here are a few techniques which you can use depending upon the situation. Practice them. After all, you probably won't be able to review this text while approaching, while looking for, or while confronting the violator.

THE FLASHLIGHT AND BLIND TECHNIQUE

One of the most widely used flash techniques is the flash and blind technique. Although primarily used at night, it can also be used during the daytime. This technique is used as follows:

1. When talking to your opponent, stand in the interrogation position (firearm away from the person) with your flashlight beam focused upon his/her chest area.

2. Hold your flashlight in your weak hand either civilian-style or police-style.

3. When necessary (the person moves toward you or you want to grasp the person), snap your weak hand wrist upward shining the light beam directly into the person's eyes. The light beam should temporarily destroy the person's night vision. The person should immediately react to the light beam by closing his/her eyes, by attempting to block the beam with a hand or by turning his/her head to avoid the light beam. After you alter his/her vision, quickly grasp the person or take other appropriate follow-up measures.

The flash and blind technique can also be used when first encountering a stranger. For example, you might be searching a building, a basement or a field when suddenly you illuminate another person. Immediately flash the light beam directly into his/her eyes. The reasons: to temporarily destroy his/her night vision; to make them react to your light beam, hopefully altering their intended thoughts and actions; and to give you time to assess the person and to plan an appropriate response.

THE FLASHLIGHT ROLL TECHNIQUE

Another widely used flashlight technique is the flashlight roll technique. This technique is primarily used to illuminate a darkened room, and should be used with a partner. You need a partner to help you look into the room, and to retrieve the flashlight when you roll it across the floor. This technique is used as follows:

1. Position yourself on the right side of the doorjamb with your partner positioned on the left side.

2. If the door is closed, open it, pushing it all the way open.

3. After the door is opened, both you and your partner should squat beside the doorjamb. Don't change positions, just squat down.

4. Hold your flashlight by the barrel, palm up--so that its head is slightly inserted in the open doorway.

5. Turn on the flashlight.

6. Simultaneously, let it roll off your fingertips and toward your partner.

7. As the flashlight rolls toward your partner, both of you should be looking into the room.

8. The two of you should be able to see what is being illuminated by the light beam.

9. When the flashlight reaches your partner, (s)he should turn it off and roll it back to you. You can then repeat the process.

10. If you're using a flashlight with an adjustable beam, such as (a) Mag-Lite, prior to rolling it, adjust the beam from spotlight to floodlight so that you can illuminate a larger area.

11. **CAUTION:** Do not stand in the doorway or enter the room while your flashlight is being rolled across the floor. The reason: if there is an armed person in the room, (s)he may shoot at the light.

12. **CAUTION:** Before you attempt this technique, make sure that your flashlight will roll smoothly across the floor. If your flashlight has a large, bulky on-off switch, it will probably not roll very smoothly. In fact, the flashlight may roll until it hits the on-off switch, change angle and illuminate you or your partner with the light beam.

13. To correct the situation described in point 12, purchase an "o" ring. (Mag-Instrument makes one or you can get one at a vacuum cleaner dealer.) The "o" ring can be attached to the head of your flashlight to raise it so that it will roll smoothly.

THE LIGHT AND PEEK TECHNIQUE

To properly use this technique, you will need two flashlights. If your partner has a flashlight use it; if not, give him/her your back-up flashlight. Here's how the light and peek technique works.

1. Position yourself on the right side of the doorjamb with your partner positioned on the left side.

2. If the door is closed, open it, pushing it all the way open.

3. After the door is opened, your partner should squat or lie prone beside the doorjamb. You should squat, too.

4. Hold the flashlight civilian-style for both safety and for flexibility.

5. Reaching upward and toward the doorway, insert your flashlight into the doorway, keeping it above the height of your partner.

7. Your partner should peek around the doorjamb looking into the room. (S)He should be able to see what is being illuminated by the light beam.

8. After (s)he has looked into the room, turn off the flashlight.

9. Repeat the technique, only this time you are the viewer. Your partner will shine his/her light into the room while you peek. If your partner is lying down, (s)he is now squatting.

10. Remember to keep the flashlight above the person who is looking into the room. Also, keep the light beam above your head, too. Doing so will help to confuse the person who might be in the room.

THE BLINK AND MOVE TECHNIQUE

Occassionally, you may find yourself in an open field, parking lot or other area where cover is not readily available. You may, therefore, be forced to use your flashlight without the aid of cover. Generally, for safety reasons, it's not a good idea to use your flashlight without first locating and using cover.

When you find yourself in this position don't start randomly blinking your flashlight to illuminate your path. Instead, perform the following steps:

1. Squat down and remain motionless. The reasons: to let your eyes adjust to the darkness and to listen for the other person's movements.

2. Assess the available light sources. Possibly there is enough moon light or street light for you to use without turning on your flashlight.

3. Make a mental note of where there are light sources. You want to make sure that you don't position yourself against them. The result: a silhouette target for your opponent.

After taking "inventory" of the available light, you determine there's insufficient light. Hence, you are forced to use your flashlight. To maximize your safety, use the blink and move technique. Here are the steps:

1. Holding your weapon in your strong hand, hold the flashlight--civilian-style--in your weak hand.

2. Squat slightly, bending your knees.

3. Assume the proper FBI night firing position. You may wish to use the other night firing techniques in Chapter XV, but remember that you're holding the flashlight in the center of your body.

4. Remember, too, to keep the head of the flashlight away from and in front of your body. The reason: to avoid illuminating you with the light beam's spillover.

5. Now, blink the light on for a second so that you can check an area. Then move when the light is turned off.

6. Don't keep the light on for any long period of time. If you do, your opponent will be able to locate you and possibly your position.

7. It should have dawned on you by now that if your flashlight doesn't have blinking capabilities, this technique won't work. Oh, and don't think you're good enough to move the on-off switch back and forth. If you drop the flashlight when it's on, it won't go out until you turn it off. In fact, it may illuminate you after landing on the ground. Conversely, should you drop your flashlight while pressing on the button to cause the light to blink, it will automatically go out.

8. Finally, should you be forced to shoot at your opponent, turn off your flashlight. The reason· so that (s)he can't locate you. The rule of thumb: shoot and then move.

The Blink and Move technique is based upon a couple of things. First, it is assumed that your opponent will shoot at the light beam. By holding the flashlight away from your body, the shot should miss you. Second, blinking the light should not give your opponent the opportunity or the time to locate you or learn your movements.

OTHER USES OF THE FLASHLIGHT

There are many other uses for your flashlight in situations where surviving is paramount. If you stop and think about the possible uses of the flashlight, you should be able to think of many more uses than are presented here.

IN EMERGENCIES

Your flashlight can be used as a splint, as a tourniquet winder or to break windows in the event of an emergency. To use as a splint, simply place it parallel to the person's arm or leg. Then wrap and/or tape it to that part of the body being immobilized. In a few rare cases you may need to remove the head of the flashlight so that the barrel can be placed evenly against the injured extremity. After the person has been admitted to the hospital, remember to recover your flashlight.

If you're the first person to arrive at a motor vehicle accident or at a home where medical help was summoned, your flashlight may come in handy. For example, if a motorist were pinned in a vehicle, you could use your flashlight (if it were heavy-duty metal) to break the door windows. To break the window, simply hit the bottom corner of the glass with the head or the tail cap of your flashlight.

A similar technique could be used if you were the first to respond to a residence where medical help was needed. For example, the doors and the windows of a house are locked. You look inside and see someone lying on the floor. Immediately, break a window with your flashlight to gain access. Again, simply strike the pane of glass with either end of your heavy-duty flashlight.

Conversely, you can use your flashlight to prevent windows and doors from being closed. You could, for example, insert the barrel of your flashlight between a door and its frame should someone attempt to slam the door in your face. You could also prevent a driver from winding up his/her window by inserting the barrel between the glass and the window frame. Be careful as you might unintentionally break the driver's window. However, it's still better and safer than getting your arm or your fingers caught between the window and its frame.

AGAINST DOGS

Your flashlight may help you if you're ever attacked by a dog. Generally, a dog will bite the closest item to him. For example, if a dog is attacking and you extend your hand and arm, he is more than likely going to bite your hand.

Knowing this, the next time a dog advances on you, offer him the flashlight by extending it toward him. Although he may rip it from your hand, it should give you time to draw your weapon or use appropriate follow-up measures.

DISTRACTION BY THROWING

Your flashlight can be thrown at an advancing person for the purposes of distracting him/her. For example, if a person were to suddenly advance toward you with a knife, throw your flashlight at him/her. This should not only distract the person causing him/her to slow down, but it should rid your hand of the flashlight. This is especially important if you are holding the flashlight in your strong hand. Free your hand, then draw your weapon.

ARM EXTENSION

Depending upon the length of your flashlight, your reach could be extended six to twenty-four-plus inches. This may become necessary if you had to break a window, break a light source or turn off a light switch all of which were beyond your arm's reach. To use the flashlight as an extension of your arm, firmly grasp it by the tail cap portion of the barrel or by its head. Then perform your desired task.

RESCUE BAR*

If your flashlight can be opened at both ends (removal of the tail cap and the head) it can be used as a rescue bar during an emergency. For example, if a child fell into a large hole, remove the tail cap section or the flashlight. Next, remove the batteries. Finally, remove the head of the flashlight.

*Developed by the Author.

Next, insert a heavy rope or a nylon cord through the hollow barrel of the flashlight. Tie one end securely to the rope. You know that you're right if the flashlight barrel looks like a tow bar used to pull water skiers.

After you have constructed the rescue bar, lower it to the child. Tell him/her to grasp the bar (flashlight barrel). Then hoist the child from the hole.

You may wish to use another flashlight to make a rescue bar at the other end of the rope. This will allow one person the opportunity to maintain a good grip on the rope. It should also eliminate rope burns to the person holding the barrel.

Finally, this technique could be used to pull a person to shore if (s)he were stranded in the water. Granted, the barrel would probably not float, but the person could more than likely retrieve it. Caution must be exercised in the throwing of the rescue bar to the person. The barrel could possibly injure the person if it were to strike the person on the face or the head.

FENCE CLIMBING

If necessary, you and a partner could scale a chain-link fence by using two flashlights. Most likely this technique would be used by the two of you when chasing another person.

Using two flashlights (yours and your partners), place one in each hand so that you are holding them by the head. Next, insert the barrel of each flashlight through the holes of the fence. Stagger the height of the flashlights in an effort to create steps. Tell you partner to place a foot on each "step", and to simultaneously grasp the fence with his/her hands. As your partner steps on the higher of the two flashlights, remove the lower flashlight, reinserting it at a higher level. After your partner has climed over the top of the fence, "walk" your partner down the "steps" by reversing the process. After your partner is safely on the other side, throw both flashlights over the fence so he can "walk" you over the fence.

One final point. Prior to leaving a darkened area and entering a brightened area, or vice versa, close one eye keeping the other eye open. After entering the contrasting illuminated area, open the closed eye. The reason: the closed eye should not be as affected with the change in illumination levels. Hence, your vision should not be as impaired as if you fail to use this technique.

In summary, your survival will depend upon many things: the proper attitude, the proper mental conditioning; the proper physical conditioning; the proper use of techniques; the proper use of tactics; and the sprinkling of luck. One important ingredients in the recipe for surviving is practice. You must practice the techniques and the tactics in this book and in other books to put the odds for surviving in your favor.

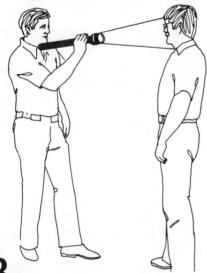

Knowledge without practice is not enough. Many studies and actual case histories have shown that when placed in a stressful situation you will use what you were taught. Therefore, practice these techniques for surviving dangerous situations until they become like your breathing--second nature.

SITUATION: You wish to temporarily destroy a person's night vision using the Flash and Blind technique.

ACTION:

1

Standing in the interrogation position (firearm away from the person) and holding the flashlight--police-style--in your right hand, you begin talking to the person. Your flashlight in on with the light beam aimed at the person's chest area. Aiming the light beam at the person's chest should illuminate the mid- and the upper portion of the person's body.

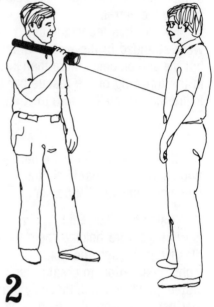

2

Should the person make a sudden movement toward you, or should you want to grasp the person, snap your wrist upward, shining the light beam directly into the person's eyes.

3

Flashing the light beam directly into the person's eyes should temporarily destroy his/her night vision. The person should immediately react to the light beam by closing his/her eyes, by attempting to block the beam with a hand or by turning his/her head to avoid the light beam. After you flash the light beam into the person's eyes, quickly grasp the person or take other appropriate follow-up measures.

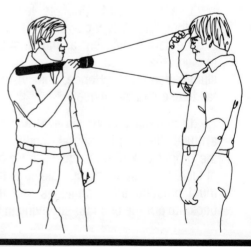

SITUATION: You and your partner decide to check a darkened room by illuminating it with the FLASHLIGHT ROLL TECHNIQUE.

ACTION:

1 Positioning yourself on the right side of the doorjamb with your partner positioned on the left side of the doorjamb, push the door all the way open. Next, both you and your partner must squat so that the two of you can use this technique. Holding your flashlight by the barrel--palm up--turn on the flashlight.

2 Simultaneously, let it roll off your fingertips and toward your partner. As the flashlight rolls toward your partner, both of you should be looking into the room. When the flashlight reaches your partner, (s)he should turn it off and roll it back to you. You can then repeat the process.

SITUATION: You and your partner must scale a fence in a yard or in an industrial area.

ACTION:
Using two flashlights (yours and your partners), place one in each hand so that you are holding them by the head. Next, insert the barrel of each flashlight through the holes of the fence. Stagger the height of the flashlights in an effort to create steps. Tell your partner to place a foot on each "step", and to simultaneously grasp the fence with his/her hands. As your partner steps on the higher of the two flashlights, remove the lower flashlight, reinserting it at a higher level. After your partner has climbed over the top of the fence, "walk" your partner down the "steps" by reversing the process. After your partner is safely on the other side, throw both flashlights over the fence so he can "walk" you over the fence.

Chapter XVII

FLASHLIGHT MAINTENANCE

If you properly care for it, your flashlight should last you for years. Granted, a plastic flashlight, because of its construction and design, may have a shorter life span than an aluminum one. However, all things being equal, the life span of most flashlights should be lengthy. There are times, however, when maintenance should and will occur.

Preventive maintenance should be done on a regular basis. The goal of preventive maintenance is to prevent problems before they develope. Here are a few tips to help you in designing your preventive maintenance program:

• Place a small amount of petroleum jelly on all threads periodically. The reasons: to prevent rust and to keep the threaded parts moving freely.

• Only use a lens cloth to clean the lens and the reflector of the flashlight. The reasons: to prevent the scratching of or the damaging of these two items.

• **DO NOT** allow your flashlight to sit for long periods of time with partially used batteries. The reason: to prevent battery leakage which will damage the flashlight.

Daily maintenance may be necessary if you use the flashlight on a daily basis. Your daily maintenance program should include the following:

• Checking the bulb to make sure that it works before taking the flashlight with you.

• Checking the batteries before you go to work to make sure that they are not dead is important, too.

If you work in the police, the fire or the emergency medical professions you constantly rely upon a flashlight. Hence, checking the batteries is as important as making sure that your firearm is loaded, that your oxygen tank has enough oxygen or that your first aid kit contains enough supplies. To check the batteries buy an inexpensive battery tester. Do it now. It could save a life: yours or someone elses.

Unfortunately, there may be times when you discover problems with your flashlight. Here is a list of the most frequent problems with "trouble shooting" corrective tips.

1. Your flashlight does not turn on or is intermittently "on".

- Check the bulb. It may be defective or be burned out.

- Check the tail cap. Make sure that it is properly and securely tightened. Look for foreign matter in the threads which would cause the tail cap not to close.

- Check the batteries. Even if the batteries are new, they could be defective or be dead.

- Check the main spring. Make sure that it isn't corroded.

- Check the positive switch contact. Make sure that it isn't corroded.

- Check all non-plated areas. If these areas are painted, corroded, etc. loss of electrical contact will result.

2. Your switch button remains down and fails to return to its "normal" postion.

- It may be the weather. Occasionally, cold weather will affect the rubber switch seal return.

- If this happens, return your flashlight to the manufacturer.

3. Your flashlight only works intermittently.

- Check the batteries. The ends of the batteries may be deformed due to compressive impacts. Hence, full contact is not made. This is the common problem when your flashlight will work in some positions but not in other positions.

- Check the batteries for cracks or distortions.
- Check the flashlight for foreign particles which may affect it from functioning properly.

- Review the steps listed under No. 1 above.

4. When you turn on the flashlight the bulb blows out immediately, or blows out within several minutes.

• Simple, it's the wrong bulb.

5. Your flashlight beam fails to focus to a spot light.

• Replace the bulb. The bulb may be defective or be the wrong bulb.

• Check the head assembly. It is possible that the head assembly is not on properly.

6. You checked the bulb, the batteries, the non-plated areas the barrel and the flashlight still doesn't work.

• If you did everything above and it still doesn't work, send the flashlight back to the manufacturer. The manufacturer will inspect it for defects.

Finally, don't play "mechanic" with your flashlight. Most, if not all, manufacturers will void your warranty if you have attempted to repair the flashlight. For example, you dismantle the switch and then decide that you can't fix it. If you damage or alter the flashlight, don't be angry when the manufacturer tells you that the warranty is void. If the flashlight doesn't work, send it back. After all, you paid for it.

Regarding batteries, should they leak and ruin your flashlight send everything to the battery manufacturer. The battery manufacturer should refund or replace your flashlight.

Chapter XVIII

SELECTED MEDICAL IMPLICATIONS OF
THE CAROTID RESTRAINT HOLD

The carotid restraint hold is one of the most effective restraint techniques taught to criminal justice personnel, and also one of the most widely abused techniques when used by these same people. While few people will question its ease of application and extreme effectiveness when used properly, there is a growing concern among judges, prosecutors, defense attorneys and even criminal justice personnel regarding its often unjustified use by street officers.

For example, an officer in the Northwestern part of the United States applied the carotid restraint hold on a driver when he refused to get into the officer's police vehicle. In another case, a correctional officer applied the restraint hold to an inmate who refused to go into his jail cell. In both cases, the victims of the carotid restraint hold died.

In reaction to the growing trend of fatal injuries caused from the application of the carotid restraint hold, many people are microscopically examining the use of this technique. One person who reviewed the use of the carotid restraint hold was U.S. District Judge Robert M. Takasugi. In a 1980 descision, Judge Takasugi said that the carotid restraint hold constituted deadly force as presently applied.

Judge Takasugi issued a preliminary injunction against the police from using the choke hold unless they are confronted by a life or death situation. Although his decision was quickly overturned, it heightened the controversy surrounding this technique. In an effort to better understand the pros and the cons surrounding this technique, let's examine it from a medical and a practical viewpoint.

Before we discuss the practical problems involving the application of the carotid restraint technique, let's first define the carotid restraint hold. When asked how the carotid restraint hold works, the average police officer will tell you that you are stopping the blood flow to the brain by pinching shut the carotid artery. When the flow of blood is stopped, the person will pass out. This description is not entirely correct.

To fully understand the effects of the carotid artery, look at Figure H-1. This figure shows the carotid arteries and the throat area. Studying this figure will help you understand how the carotid restraint hold works.

FIGURE H-1

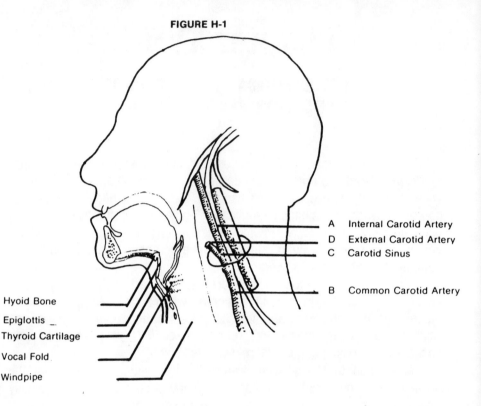

A   Internal Carotid Artery
D   External Carotid Artery
C   Carotid Sinus

B   Common Carotid Artery

E   Hyoid Bone
F   Epiglottis
G   Thyroid Cartilage
H   Vocal Fold
I   Windpipe

FIGURE T-1

A   Greater Cornu of Hyoid

B   Body of Hyoid

C   Thyroid Cartilage

D   Inferior Cornu of Hyoid

E   Cricoid Cartilage

F   Trachia

First, blood containing the necessary oxygen is supplied to your head by the common carotid artery and the vertebral artery. Located on each side of your neck, the two common arteries are connected to the large aorta of the heart. At approximately the height of your Adam's Apple, the artery divides into the external and internal carotid arteries.

Blood is supplied to your face and to your scalp by the external carotid artery, while the internal carotid artery supplies blood to your brain and to your eyes.

Part C on Figure H-1 shows where the carotid artery divides into two parts: part A, the internal carotid artery and part B, the external carotid artery. Where this split takes place is known as the carotid sinus. The carotid sinus will be discussed later.

In addition to the carotid arteries, there are two vertebral arteries which arise from the subclavian arteries. The vertebral arteries are located in the neck and supplement the flow of blood to the brain.

Two large internal jugular veins—one one each side of your neck—carry deoxygenated blood from the brain. The blood flows down your internal jugular veins and is carried back to the heart by other smaller veins. Blood is also collected from other parts of your head by smaller external jugular veins.

This network of arteries and veins contradicts most officer's statements regarding the pinching shut of the carotid artery. As shown, the mere pinching shut of the common carotid artery or the internal carotid arteries does not completely stop the blood flow to the brain. The reason: blood is supplied to the brain via the vertebral arteries. However, pressure on the carotid sinus can produce the responses generally credited to pressing on the carotid artery.

Pressure applied on the carotid sinus generally results in a slowing of the heart. The carotid sinus nerve causes the vagus nerve to engage which causes a person's blood pressure to drop. As a result the brain is not supplied enough oxygen, causing the victim to faint.

Another method to cause a person to faint is through respiratory strangulation. Basically, all you must do is press against the trachia so that the person cannot breath. Unconsciousness will take effect within three minutes.

While few officers would admit to intentionally stranguling a person, a substantial number of "choke-out" deaths are in fact caused by suffocation. While the officer doesn't intend for it to happen, sometimes it cannot be avoided.

For example, while attending the police academy your defensive tactics instructor taught your class the carotid restraint technique. It was shown to you and then you applied it to a classmate who wasn't fighting or struggling. It worked and seemed easy to apply. However, on the street in an actual confrontation the application of the technique isn't so easy.

One of the problems in applying the carotid restraint hold is that the suspect isn't standing still. Instead of cooperating, (s)he is struggling. Hence, when you attempt to apply the carotid restraint hold to the side of the person's neck, your flashlight is suddenly against the person's larynx. Unknowingly, you forcefully squeeze your flashlight against the person's throat, breaking the hyoid bone. Within three minutes the person dies from suffocation.

In his book, FUNDAMENTALS OF MODERN POLICE IMPACT WEAPONS, Massad Ayoob mentions some physical after-effects the victim of a carotid restriant of choke hold may develop. For example, some people will vomit when they come too, and may be disoriented for a period of time. There are other possible effects, too.

Ayoob is quick to mention that he sought out a neurosurgeon, a cardiologist, an opthamologist and a specialist in internal medicine to comment on the after-effect of the technique in question. According to Ayoob, all of the doctors were familiar with the various choke-out techniques. They said that a certain percentage of victims would suffer the following: a heart attack; convulsive seizures; aspiration of vomit; blindness; ruptured arteries; permanent brain damage; and/or spinal injury. These after effects are also supported in whole or in part by other medical professionals and researchers.

For these and other reasons too numerous to discuss, I recommend that the carotid restraint hold not be taught to officers. I agree that the technique will work, but I also agree that the medical implications and the apparent inability of the officer to prudently and judiciously use this technique mandates its deletion from a basic course in defensive tactics.

Chapter XIX

FLASHLIGHTS AND THE LAW

When I conceived the idea for this book in 1980, I decided to include a section on flashlight law; that is, court cases which examined the use of force where the flashlight was the primary impact tool used in self-defense or used in the effecting of an arrest. The reason: most everyone knows of a couple incidents where the flashlight was used as a so-called defensive impact tool, but few people actually knew the case situation or the events surrounding the case. Hence, I set out to discover the facts. However, I didn't think that it would be as difficult of a task to locate the information as it turned out to be.

After consulting many police attorneys, police administrators, police researchers, general-practice attorneys and others regarding flashlight case law, most of them said the same thing: "There's a lot of flashlight case law out there, but no one has ever collected it...Good luck."

Well, luck came my way when I started to receive a few case citations from various people. Armed with these "leads" plus the spending of countless hours in the Boston University Law School library, this chapter was given birth. To the best of my knowledge, this chapter contains the most flashlight cases ever to be presented and then discussed between two covers, with the exception of course, of law books.

Please note that many of the more celebrated flashlight cases have not been cited in this chapter. The reasons: most, if not all of these cases, are still being appealed or the defendants are involved in civil litigation; and, should the case be overturned on appeal, the information contained in this chapter would misinform you. Therefore, to avoid the possibility of prejudicing these cases for either side by commenting on them, only those cases which have been fully adjudicated or settled out of court are presented and discussed.

Before we go any farther, I want to acknowledge the kindness of a few folks who helped to make this chapter a reality. Although they provided input and other forms of assistance, any errors or omissions are totally my responsibility. Many thanks to these folks: Dennis Anderson, Calibre Press, Inc., Joe Scuro, Esq., Nicholas and Barrera, Howard Berringer, Americans for Effective Law Enforcement; Arnold Bernstein, Albuquerque Police Department; Vernon Turner, Albuquerque City Claims; Massad Ayoob, Lethal Force Institute; John Farnam, Defense Training; Denny Fallon, National Media Group; Special Agent John Desmedt, United States Secret Service; and J. David Myers, reknowned combat instructor.

USE OF FORCE

All of us must abide by certain laws in the United States. Although there are many categories of law with which we must live, this chapter will only focus upon two of these categories: criminal laws and civil laws. For example, if you as a police officer violate a person's civil rights under 42 USC $ 1983, this is a violation in the criminal law category. If, however, you commit a tort (or wrong) you now enter the category of civil law. And, it's possible to have committed an act which falls into both categories, and, in most cases, the injuried party has a right to seek a legal remedy through the courts.

What we're really discussing in this chapter is your legitimate use of force. At the end of the chapter the focus will be upon the use of force with a flashlight. For example, if you, as a police officer, use too much force to subdue a violator or to defend yourself, you may have violated a criminal law, or you could be sued civilly for your actions or your failure to act. Therefore, let's examine the various stages of force, first beginning our discussion with the disparity of force concept.

DISPARITY OF FORCE

Generally, whether you're a civilian or a police officer, you can only use that amount of force which is necessary to defend yourself or to arrest a violator. Too much force and you may have violated the law or the violator's rights; too little force and you might be crippled for life or be killed from the violator's attack.

In essence, when discussing the disparity of force concept, the focus is upon your not exceeding the violator's force which (s)he is using or threatening to use against you. For example, if the violator is aiming a revolver at you, you can, most likely, legitimately use deadly force as a countermeasure. However, if a person only gives you the finger and your response is to grab the finger and proceed to break it, you have probably used too much force. Although you may feel better having relieved your tension, the injured person may have you arrested for assault and battery, may sue you civilly for damages or may do both. Hence, it's important for you to understand what you can and can't do, when it comes to the use of legitimate force.

Now, let's make one thing clear right now. The laws governing your use of legitimate force are not black and white. At best, they are grey. When the violator is armed and threatening you with death or great bodily harm and you respond with deadly force, the issue appears to be much more clear. The violator threatened to kill you; hence, your response--deadly force--will probably be viewed as legitimate and as appropriate. However, what about the situation where you are confronted by an unarmed violator.

Generally, there are two measures used by the court to determine the disparity of force in such situations. They are:

1. The strength, age, size, etc. of your attacker compared to your strength, age, size, etc.
2. The number of people who attacked you.

For example, if you are a small male, say 4 foot 9, and you're attacked by a 200-pound, 6 foot 3 male who is in good physical shape, you can probably justify your use of force response. However, if the reverse were true, you might not be able to justify your actions. And, if you're both the same size, age, etc. --how are you now going to justify your actions. As you can see, there are many variables to be factored into the use of force equation. And, it would help if there were a chart to help you decide your chances of survival against someone smaller, larger or the same size as you.

Exhibit 19-1 is an attempt to illustrate your chances of survival when confronted by various sized attackers. As noted, the assumption is that both you and your attacker have the same amount of training or equipment. Of course, if one of you has a firearm, this chart will not be as accurate. Prepared by noted combat instructor and researcher, J. David Myers, Exhibit 19-1 attempts to show you your chances of surviving an attack by various sized assailants. To read the chart, simply locate your size (i.e., mini, small, medium, large, monster) and then read across the chart to discover your chances of survival. The first number shown is the odds (percentage) of your surviving an attack by the size of person indicated above the number. As you can see, there are no 100% chances of surviving.

Coupled with Exhibit 19-1, there are four elements which must also be present, especially to justify your use of deadly force. For the sake of discussion, let's use deadly force as the common denominator. After building a solid foundation in this area, the escalation and the de-escalation of force as it applies to various situations will be discussed.

According to John Farnam, noted weapons instructor, there are four elements which must be present before you can legitimately use deadly force. If all of these elements are present, you will, most likely, be able to "justify" your defensive response. The four elements are:

1. Ability
2. Opportunity
3. Imminent Jeopardy
4. Preclusion

Ability simply means that the violator possesses the ability to kill you or to cause you serious bodily harm. The fact that the violator said that

EXHIBIT 19-1

	MINI	SMALL	MEDIUM	LARGE	MONSTER
MINI	50 / 50	40 / 60	30 / 70	20 / 80	10 / 90
SMALL	60 / 40	50 / 50	40 / 60	30 / 70	20 / 80
MEDIUM	70 / 30	60 / 40	50 / 50	40 / 60	30 / 70
LARGE	80 / 20	70 / 30	60 / 40	50 / 50	40 / 60
MONSTER	90 / 10	80 / 20	70 / 30	60 / 40	50 / 50

MINI — Under 5 Ft. — Under 100 Lb.
SMALL — 5 Ft. to 5 Ft. 6 In. — 100 to 150 Lb.
MEDIUM — 5 Ft. 6 In. to 6 Ft. — 150 to 200 Lb.
LARGE — 6 Ft. to 6 Ft. 6 In. — 200 to 250 Lb.
MONSTER — Over 6 Ft. 6 In. — Over 250 Lb.

NOTE: In a head-on confrontation your chances of survival depend to a great extent on the size difference between you and your opponent. This assumes equal training and equipment. The exception is Handgun Fighting.

(s)he is going to kill you isn't good enough. The violator must be able to carry out the threat. For example, a quadraplegic who says that (s)he is going to beat you to death with an iron pipe, probably doesn't possess the ability to carry out the threat.

Opportunity is the second element. If the violator doesn't have the opportunity to kill you or to cause you great bodily harm, you will probably not be justified in using deadly or excessive force. For example, a person who is holding a hatchet and who is standing 40 yards away doesn't have the opportunity to use his hatchet on you.

Imminent jeopardy is the third element. You must be placed in immediate jeopardy or your claim of self-defense may not be valid. Referring to the previous example, a person who is standing 40 yards away from you and holding a hatchet doesn't place you in imminent jeopardy. If he were holding a rifle, it may be a different story.

Preclusion is the final element. Preclusion simply means that you reasonably exhausted all your avenues of retreat at the time and place. In essence, your defensive actions were the only option that you had.

Paying lip service to these elements isn't good enough to justify your actions. You must have been in imminent jeopardy, have exhausted all your options but the one that you used, and your attacker must have possessed both the ability and the opportunity to have killed or to have seriously injured you.

So far we have only addressed deadly force encounters. You must understand this area especially when you consider the numerous incidents where people have been severely injured or even killed after being struck on top of the head with a flashlight. Now that you have a general idea about what's needed to justify deadly force, let's examine a more generalized use of force situation.

Exhibit 19-2 shows continium of force which we shall use to discuss the concept of escalation of force.

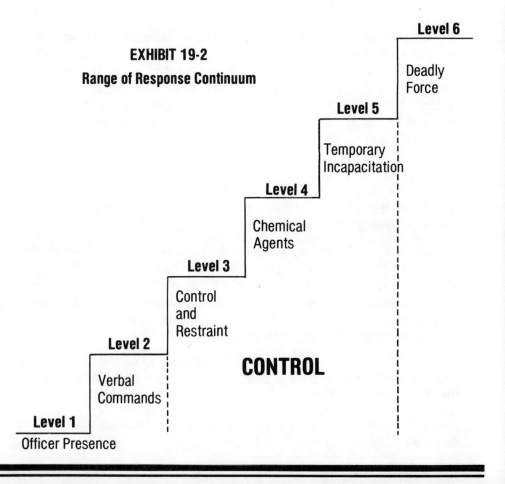

EXHIBIT 19-2

Range of Response Continuum

Level 6

Deadly Force

Level 5

Temporary Incapacitation

Level 4

Chemical Agents

Level 3

Control and Restraint

CONTROL

Level 2

Verbal Commands

Level 1

Officer Presence

ESCALATION OF FORCE

Exhibit 19-2 is an attempt to make tangible an intangible (use of force). Although the shift in levels of force isn't as clear-cut as this, it will provide us with a starting point. And our focus will be upon the response of a police officer to the actions of a violator.

Level I, or officer presence, is best illustrated when the officer arrives at the scene. The violator sees the officer and does not alter his/her behavior. The assumption is that the violator knows that the person who has just arrived at the scene is a police officer. (S)He may acknowledge the officer's presence because of the marked patrol car or because of the officer's uniform. Should the violator continue his/her action, the officer may advance--or escalate--to Level II.

Level II, or verbal commands, is best illustrated when the officer advises the violator to keep quiet, move along and so forth. Again, the violator ignores the officer's verbal directions. The assumption is that the violator can clearly here the officer's directions. Should the violator continue his/her actions, the officer may advance--or escalate--to Level III.

Level III, or Control and Restraint, is best illustrated when the officer applies a defensive wrist lock or flashlight technique to control and/or restrain the violator. For example, a driver will not exit his/her car after being told to do so by the officer. Upon refusal, the officer applies a vehicle extraction technique using the flashlight. Should the violator continue his/her actions or become more violent, the officer may advance-- or escalate--to Level IV.

Level IV, or Chemical Agents, is best illustrated when the officer administers mace or a similar chemical agent to the violator. Should the violator continue his/her actions or become more violent the officer may advance--or escalate--to Level V.

Level V, or Temporary Incapacitation, is best illustrated when the officer is forced to defensively strike the violator with the flashlight. Possibly, the strike will result in the fracture of the violator's arm, thus causing temporary incapacitation. Should the violator pull a knife, draw a firearm or attempt to otherwise kill or seriously injure the officer, the officer may advance--or escalate--to Level VI.

Level VI, or Deadly Force, is best illustrated when the officer must shoot the violator, or in a life or death situation strike the violator on top of the head with a flashlight which results in the violator's death or serious injury.

It should be noted that the officer is not obligated to move onto the next level. (S)He may decide to retreat, decide to request assistance or decide upon another course of action. However, should the officer adapt his/her force to match the violators use of force, this is called **escalation.** Should the officer move downward on this scale, it is called **de-escalation.**

De-escalation may occure at any time. For example, if the officer applied a flashlight restraint technique at Level III and the violator stopped fighting and agreed to be peaceful, the officer would, most likely, be in error should (s)he continue to Levels IV, V or VI. The reason: after the violator's actions plateau or decrease in intensity, any further escalation of force on the officer's part may be viewed as excessive in nature.

Exhibit 19-3 shows the escalation of force as a straight line, rather than as a staircase. As you can see, as the violator's use of force increases, so may the officer's use of force.

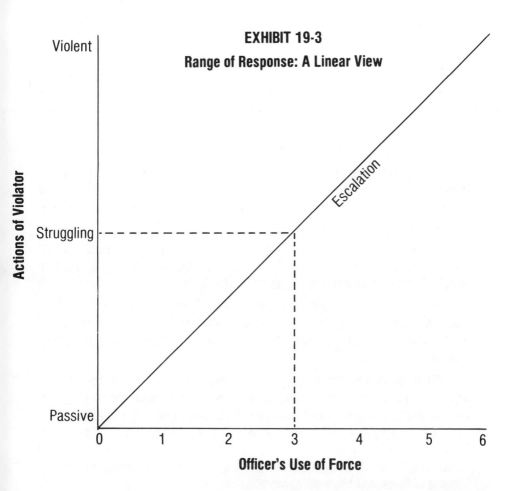

EXHIBIT 19-3

Range of Response: A Linear View

Exhibit 19-4 shows the escalation and the de-escalation of force. For example, if the violator agrees to go along peacefully at Level III, then the officer begins his/her de-escalation of force. This, however, is not to say the officer is totally relaxed and is not anticipating or aware of danger.

EXHIBIT 19-4
Escalation/De-escalation Graph

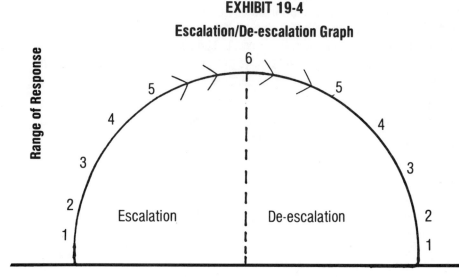

USE OF FORCE COMBINATIONS

As a police officer, a police administrator or a civilian you may be thinking that the decision to use "X" force is as clear-cut as shown in the previous exhibits. As previously mentioned, it's not simple at all. In fact, it's generally a very complex decision.

For example, Exhibit 19-5 uses a Venn diagram to illustrate the interlocking of the six levels of force. As you can see, making a decision about which level of force to use is not a simple task.

Assessing the degree of force is not always an easy task. Exhibit 19-6 using Network Analysis is a graphic illustration of how many choices you, as a police officer, have available. As shown, you have 30 combinations from which to select.

Since I advanced this concept, let me explain it. It is simply based upon what is called Network Analysis. Basically, it shows the number of combinations that are available to you. As shown, you can escalate from 1 to 2; 1 to 3; 1 to 4; 1 to 5; 1 to 6; 2 to 3; 2 to 4; 2 to 5; 2 to 6; 3 to 4; 3 to 5; 3 to 6; 4 to 5; 4 to 6; or 5 to 6. On the escalation side of the use of force, you have 15 combinations. Likewise, on the de-escalation side of the use of force you have 15 combinations.

EXHIBIT 19-5

Venn Diagram Showing the Interrelatedness of the Six Ranges of Response Levels

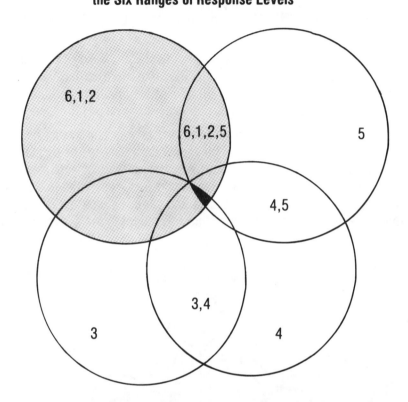

Another way to compute this is statistically using what is called a permutation. A permutation is simply a mathematical way to determine the number of combinations in a given task. Exhibit 19-7 explains the mathematics of this concept, should this be of interest to you.

For a more detailed explanation on the use of force in general or in specific situations consult your private or agency legal counsel. (S)He can more accurately advise you about the ramifications of your actions with regard to common law, state or federal statutes.

Coupled with the statutes and case law regarding the use of force and subsequently the use of the flashlight, another paralleling issue must be discussed: Agency policy governing the use of the flashlight.

FLASHLIGHT POLICY

Most everytime a police officer strikes another person with a flashlight, the violator's attorney demands to see the flashlight policy of the officer's agency. The reason: the attorney speculates that the agency's policy governing the flashlight either doesn't exist, or if it does exist, it's very restrictive or it doesn't cover the use of the flashlight as a defensive impact tool. Hence, the agency's policy will probably do more harm than good to both the agency and to the officer when it is admitted as evidence during the violator's trial.

Yes, that's right, your agency's flashlight policy, its rules and regulations, its procedures and similar documents regarding the use of the flashlight and other impact tools are admissible in court. And the fact that your agency doesn't have a policy in these areas will be introduced, too.

Written policies, rules, regulations, procedures and similar documents are generally developed by the administration to help standardize procedures; to help the agency accomplish its objectives; to help administer discipline; and to help the employees know what is expected of them. Historically, too, these policies and such required that the agency's employees adhere to a higher standard of conduct than the average citizen.

EXHIBIT 19-6
USE OF FORCE VIA

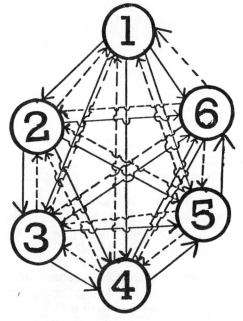

NETWORK ANALYSIS
—30 COMBINATIONS—

_____ ESCALATION OF FORCE
----------------------- DE-ESCALATION OF FORCE

In recent years, these same guidelines which were designed to help the employee and the agency are now, in certain cases, becoming a hinderance. Directives which are written by administrators without regard to existing laws or court decisions are now, in many instances, being used as a weapon against the promulgators of these rules. Gone are the days when administrators can write and then issue directives to fulfill a particular personal need. Today, the need is to write and to issue prudent guidelines which enable the administration to maintain its managerial ability, yet enables the employee to exercise judgment in the impending situation.

Unfortunately, written directives which are issued by the administration are not deemed "constitutional" just as laws are not until a guideline or law is challanged. Therefore, it is imperative that the administrator seek legal counsel **prior** to the issuing of agency guidelines which will directly or indirectly affect the behavior of employees.

EXHIBIT 19-7

MATHEMATICAL EXPLANATION OF EXHIBIT 19-6

There are six possible response levels which you can select. The sum of these alternatives is represented by N. Since you are going to move from one alternative, or level, to another, you are really taking two options at a time. These two options are represented by R. To compute the number of options that you have, we use what is called a factorial. A factorial is computed by taking the number (N) times each number behind it until we reach the number one. Hence, a six factorial means: 6 x 5 x 4 x 3 x 2 x 1 or the number 720. Since we are taking the alternatives two at a time, we subtract two from six and get four. Since we need another factorial, we take 4 x 3 x 2 x 1 and get the number 24. When we divide 720 by 24, we get 30, or the total number of range of response combinations.

Mathematically this can be expressed as:

$$\frac{N!}{(N-R)!} = \frac{6!}{(6-2)!} = \frac{720}{24} = 30$$

THE CALIFORNIA RULE

There have been precedents established regarding the admissibility of agency's written directives. One example is taken from **Dillenbeck v. City of Los Angeles,** 468 P. 2d 129 (1968) where a police officer was involved in a fatal accident. In this instance the plaintiff sought to have the department's training bulletin introduced as evidence. The training bulletin instructed officers to enter intersections at 15 miles per hour when traveling against a red light in response to an emergency call. The court admitted the bulletin to be introduced as evidence.

In 1970, again the court ruled that a department's operational and tactical manual is admissible --**Grudt v. City of Los Angeles,** 468 P. 2d 825.

These two cases, having established and reinforced the precedent of the admissibility or written directives, have come to be known as the "California Rule". A similar decision to admit departmental rules was also rendered in **DeLong v. City and County of Denver,** 530 P. 2d 1308 (1974).

On the surface it may appear that written directives can only get one into difficulty. Admittedly, they can place the administrator or the employee in jeopardy, but I believe the lack of written guidelines places everyone in even greater jeopardy. Without written directives there may exist among employees the feeling that there is no standard by which they can or will be judged. For example, should an employee be questioned about his/her use of force in a particular incident by defense counsel, what guidelines can (s)he say were followed. Having written guidelines establishes direction and standards that employees can be measured against and should use if possible. Whenever possible, the directives should have a "vent clause" for those situations which do not conform to the guidelines.

FLASHLIGHT POLICY

The following is an example of a flashlight policy.

A. The five-cell Mag-Lite Rechargeable flashlight is to be generally used as an illumination device. When needed, the Mag-Lite Rechargeable flashlight may also provide the officer with a means by which to defend himself/herself or a third party from bodily harm. It may also provide the officer with a means of restraining and of controlling passive or violent persons. The Mag-Lite Rechargeable flashlight may be used in in those situations when the firearm isn't warranted, or when the officer cannot safely obtain his/her baton or firearm. Although the Mag-Lite Rechargeable flashlight was not intended to replace the baton or the firearm, the Mag-Lite Rechargeable flashlight may be used to effect the arrest or to subdue violent persons when other means have failed or are considered impractical.

B. Those officers who are not issued the five-cell Mag-Lite Rechargeable flashlight are authorized to use a push-button flashlight constructed of aluminum, with a pre-battery weight not to exceed 24 ounces.

C. Except in those circumstances where an officer's life or the life of another person is in danger, officers may only use the flashlight as an impact tool after completing and demonstrating competency in the **YOUR AGENCY'S** certified defensive flashlight training course.

D. After the officer has been issued and has demonstrated competency in flashlight, the baton and the firearm, all other instruments of self-defense will be strictly prohibited.

FLASHLIGHT PROCEDURE

The following is an example of a flashlight procedure.

A. After exiting the vehicle, the officer shall carry the flashlight in the flashlight belt ring, unless the flashlight is being used by the officer.

B. When seated in the police vehicle, the flashlight shall be securely placed in the installed flashlight charger unit.

FLASHLIGHT REGULATIONS

The following is an example of a flashlight regulation.

A. An officer **shall not** deliberately strike another person on the head, in the groin or in the solar plexus, in the kidneys or on the spinal column **unless** the officer's life or the life of a third party is threatened.

REPORTING FLASHLIGHT USAGE

The following is an example of a flashlight usage report regulation.

A. When an officer uses the flashlight for other than illumination purposes, (s)he will make a written report which shall be submitted to his/her supervisor prior to the tour of duty's end.

GENERAL COMMENTS

Creating, implementing, enforcing and evaluating directives is a full-time job. Yet, many administrators do not recognize or refuse to recognize the importance of up-to-date, enforceable and legal directives.

In an attempt to explain the above directives, let's examine the criteria needed for good directives. Directives should meet the following criteria:

1. Directives should be legal. If they are not, you're opening the door for a suit. Hence, as previously mentioned, seek legal assistance before you issue the directives.

2. Directives should be clear. If the language of the directive isn't clear and doesn't convey the meaning which you originally intended it too, people may have difficulty following it.

3. Directives should be concise. The directives should be brief and to the point. The more words, the more room for misinterpretation.

4. Directives should be consistent. The use of flashlights would be in concert with the use of other impact tools. The reason: to reduce confusion and to maintain consistency.

5. Directives should be complete. If they aren't, the employee may be forced into making a decision that (s)he isn't capable of making. Again, when possible, the directives should contain a "vent clause" which allows the officer some flexibility.

6. Directives should be capable of being obeyed. For example, some agencies flashlight policies state that the flashlight shall not be used as an impact tool. Well, if the officer is on a vehicle stop at night and is holding a flashlight when the violator attacks, I bet the officer will be forced to disobey this inflexible directive when (s)he reacts defensively with the flashlight.

7. Coupled with the above, directives should be enforceable. It's simple. If a directive cannot be enforced, it shouldn't be issued.

Directives can also be used to motivate employees. For instance, in the previous example of flashlight policy, section C, for officers to legitimately use the flashlight as an impact tool, they must first pass a training program. and not just anyone's--the department's.

This is important for two reasons. First, by having them pass the department's training program, standardization should be achieved. That is, 20 officers are not trained by the local martial art expert, while everyone else is trained by the department. Second, such in-house training, many times produces a "hidden supervisor" aura. The officer knows that the administration is aware that (s)he completed the training, and therefore, it knows that the flashlight guidelines were presented and learned. Hence, the officer can no longer claim that (s)he wasn't familiar with the flashlight policy.

FLASHLIGHT CASES

The following are true cases where officers allegedly used a flashlight to subdue the violator. As you read each case, think of how the situation may have been handled with a knowledge of the techniques contained in this book. Also, think about the role directives would have played in each case. Finally, I think that you'll agree that professional training in the defensive uses of the flashlight may have prevented most, if not all, of these cases. As you will see, it wasn't the flashlight that hit the violator, but rather the officer who was holding the flashlight.

STATE v. LINVILLE 273 Pacific Reporter 338 (1928)

S. C. Linville was a state prohibition officer who was charged with his partner, L. L. McBride, of assault with a dangerous weapon on John W. Dennis. Dennis was allegedly struck after he refused to exit his vehicle, and after he attempted to strike Linville. The charge was as follows, to wit:

"An electric flash-light, said electric flash-light consisting of a metal and glass case, enclosing electric batteries, being cylindrical in form, of a length of twelve inches more or less, and of a weight of two pounds more or less, by then and there striking, beating and bruising said John W. Dennis about the face and head with said weapon, and said weapon as so used in said assault was and is a dangerous weapon, contrary to the statutes," etc.

In the lower court, McBride was acquitted; Linville was convicted and fined $250. On appeal Linville's conviction was reversed and the cause demanded for a new trial. In part, the court stated that it is the policy of the state to clothe its servants...an officer is not bound to submit to unreasonable and unnecessary violence and may defend himself against the same without being guilty of assault.

WENDELBOE v. JACOBSON
ET AL. 353 Pacific Reporter, 2d Series 178 (1960)

When the alleged incident occurred, Richard B. Jacobson, Billie Joe Lang and John R. Douglas were Salt Lake City, Utah police officers. The plaintiff, Stratford L. Wendelboe, placed the following action against these officers: Action for assault and battery, for false arrest and imprisonment and for malicious prosecution.

The reported facts of the incident are as follows. On April 6, 1958, at approximately three o'clock in the morning the above three police officers were on patrol in Salt Lake City. The officers noticed a vehicle parked near a service station which was under construction. They also noticed that the vehicle's lights were out and that the vehicle's engine was running.

Officer Jacobson approached the vehicle and asked the operator for his driver's license. The driver gave the officer a temporary driving permit. The officer then asked for something which listed or indicated the driver's description, as the temporary driving permit did not contain this information. The officer, seeing an army identification card, requested it. The driver refused to present the card. Officer Jacobson's suspicions aroused, the driver was asked to step out of the car where he was asked what he was doing in that location. The driver's response was: "None of your damn business. I am a citizen and have my rights." The driver was then searched and placed into the police car.

The officers advised Wendelboe that he must either identify himself to the officers' satisfaction and produce a vehicle registration certificate, or they would take him to jail. According to the officers' testimony, Wendelboe refused to answer questions and persisted to exit the police vehicle. Officer Lang found it necessary to hold on to him. Jacobson advised Lang that Wendelboe might tell them why he was there and produce identification if he were released. As the door was released, Wendelboe burst out knocking them aside. He also began to struggle with the officers and tried to break away. The officers attempted to handcuff Wendelboe. During the struggle blows were struck. After the officers secured a handcuff on Wendelboe, he flailed with it and cut Officer Jacobson. Officer Lang then struck Wendelboe on the head with a flashlight. This action helped the officers to handcuff Wendelboe. Wendelboe was charged with vagrancy, assault and battery and resisting an officer. Officer Jacobson signed the complaints.

On appeal in the Supreme Court of Utah, the court affirmed the lower court decision. That is, the officers had authority and positive absolute duty to investigate the circumstances; the officers had an absolute duty to approach the plaintiff and ask him what he was doing; and that the officers had right and duty to use such force as was reasonably necessary to complete the arrest and to detain, book and charge the accused. Further, Wendelboe could not recover for alleged assault and battery in resisting. Finally, the court awarded a judgment to the officers for attorney fees.

McCLUSKEY v. STEINHORST,
ET AL., 173 NW Reporter, 2d Series 148 (1970)

When the alleged incidents occurred, Robert Steinhorst and Dale Thieding were Sauk County deputy sheriffs. The plaintiff, Robert McCluskey placed the following action against the deputies: Action for assault and battery.

The reported facts of the incident are as follows. The deputies went to McCluskey's farm about one o'clock in the morning on July 8, 1963 after talking to Clifford Fry at the Reedsburg Hospital. Fry told them that he had taken McCluskey to his parent's home. When they arrived, McCluskey struck Fry with a board, producing cuts over Fry's left eye.

Upon arrival at McCluskey's home, the deputies were admitted by his mother. They saw McCluskey lying on a daybed wearing trousers. He appeared to be sleeping. The deputies were unsuccessful in arousing him by calling his name, but they were successful after pinching his nostrils with a thumb and forefinger. When the deputies asked McCluskey about the incident, he responded with obscenities. When the deputies told McCluskey that he was under arrest for disorderly conduct and that they were taking him to jail, he sprang off the bed swinging his fists.

During the trial Lawrence McCluskey, the plaintiff's father, told another version of the incident. He stated that on the night of the incident he came out of his bedroom after hearing the deputies in the dining room. He saw the deputies handcuff his son and then slap him hard, but his son didn't waken. Then, the deputies hit and "pounded" his son on the head and face with a flashlight three times as he lay on the daybed. His son was then allegedly pulled off or rolled off the bed onto the floor, where the deputies kicked him and then dragged him to the patrol car. The blows to the son's face broke his nose and there was a lot of blood on the floor and on the daybed. Pictures which were admitted into evidence substantiated this fact.

The plaintiff testified that he woke up on the floor and was being kicked by the deputies. He asked them to stop. He then testified that the deputies then dragged him to the patrol car and took him to jail. The next afternoon he was released from jail. He was then taken to a hospital where he stayed from July 8 through July 15. Doctors also testified about the plaintiff's injuries.

The lower court found that the deputies used excessive force in making the lawful arrest for disorderly conduct. In the jury trial, the plaintiff was awarded $5,000 compensatory damages. The jury also found that the deputies had not acted with malice and no punitive damages were awarded. On appeal by the deputies, the lower court's judgment was affirmed.

RODRIGUEZ v. CITY OF ALBUQUERQUE ET AL. (1977)

When the alleged incident occurred James M. Babich and Ronald Wuenschel were police officers for the city of Albuquerque.

Although a court record could not be located in this case, the reported facts are as follows. On November 10. 1977 Officer Babich and Wuenschel were dispatched to an alleged family fight. A Mrs. Rodriguez had requested help at the address she gave dispatch.

Upon arrival, the officers allegedly found Andrew Ramirez arguing with his sister, Trini Ramirez. The mother, Maria Rodriguez, told the officers that she wanted Andrew to leave. After the officers failed to calm down Andrew and convince him to leave voluntarily, an altercation developed. During the altercation, Officer Babich struck Andrew on the head with a flashlight. Andrew's younger brother, Antonio, allegedly entered the altercation and was arrested for interferring with the officers in resisting arrest by Officer Wuenschel.

Unconscious, Andrew was taken outside where rescue and ambulance personnel were called. Andrew was taken to a local hospital where he was pronounced dead. The preliminary autopsy report indicated death was **possibly** caused by a blow to the head.

Although it was never proven that the blow to Andrew's head definitely killed him, an award of $68,000 was declared and issued.

UNITED STATES OF AMERICA v. MARVIS RICHARD HOGAN
(Sixth Circuit Court of Appeals, No. 77-5061; 1977).

When the alleged incident occurred, Marvis Richard Hogan was a police officer for the city of Scottsville, Kentucky. The plaintiff, United States of America, placed the following action against the officer: that he violated 18 U.S.C. $ 242 with death resulting.

The reported facts of the incident are as follows. On September 28, 1974 the officer was dispatched by radio to investigate a complaint of Marie Stewart--which was made by telephone at 7:23 p.m.--that a person was driving in a reckless manner in a described location. Officer Hogan arrived at approximately 7:30 p.m. siren on and lights flashing. In uniform, Officer Hogan exited his patrol car carrying a combination flashlight and nightstick. Prior to the officer's arrival, the driver had parked the car he had been driving and had proceeded across the street to his mobile home trailer.

Upon arrival of the officer, the driver, Larry Blankenship walked from his trailer toward the officer who was approaching him. Several witnesses testified that Blankenship did not appear to be drunk, did not stagger or stumble and walked normally.

Standing approximately two to three feet apart and facing one another, Hogan advised Blankenship that he was under arrest as a public drunk for disorderly conduct. Blankenship voiced his refusal to be arrested. Hogan then told Blankenship that he would have to come along or he would be hurt. Blankenship, according to Hogan, jerked away, stepped back, doubled his fist and again voiced resistance. Hogan, in order to defend himself, by not affording Blankenship an opportunity to strike first, hit him hard with the flashlight-nightstick. The blow was to the left side of Blankenship's head, and was the only blow which he received. The witnesses testified that the blow was very loud, like a gunshot.

The witnesses testified that the confrontation lasted approximately five to fifteen seconds. All the witnesses also testified that Blankenship was unarmed and had his hands to his side at all times; that he made no movement at all prior to being hit; that Hogan did not reach for or grab Blankenship; that Blankenship did not jerk away, pull back, double his fist or re-position his hands or body in any way; and that Blankenship made no threatening gestures.

After Blankenship was struck, he fell to the ground. Hogan walked to his police car and when he returned Blankenship was gone. Apparently, Blankenship got up and went to his father-in-law's home. This was shortly after 8:00 p.m. He remained there for approximately ten minutes. He lost consciousness shortly after his arrival. Blankenship was taken to the Allen County Memorial Hospital at 8:23 p.m., where he was examined and admitted. Approximately 12 a.m. his condition deteriorated; he was transferred to Vanderbilt Hospital for neurosurgery. Unconscious and near-death upon his arrival, he was suffering from pressure on the brain resulting from the formation of a blood clot underneath the skull fracture on the left side of the skull. Transferred to another hospital on April 9, 1975 Blankenship died on April 12, 1975 as a result of brain damage caused by Hogan's blow.

The court found Hogan guilty and ordered him to serve five (5) years. On appeal, the court affirmed the verdict.

ANZURES v. CITY OF ALBUQUERQUE, ET AL.
(Second Judicial District, Case No.: 79-01180)

When the alleged incident occurred William Middleton was a police officer for the city of Albuquerque. The plaintiff, Alfred Anzures, placed the following action against the city, the officer and the police chief: assault and battery.

The reported facts of the incident are as follows. On or about August 20, 1978 at approximately 2:00 a.m., Officer Middleton saw the plaintiff "slide" through a red light. After stopping the defendant, the officer stated that he was going to cite the plaintiff for a red light violation, for speed too fast for conditions and for an expired driver's license. After reading the citations, the plaintiff said that he disagreed with the statement of facts, and refused to sign the citations. The plaintiff was then arrested.

According to the plaintiff, the officer told him to leave his vehicle, walk to the front of it, place both hands on the hood while bending over the hood of the automobile in a forward position from the waist. The plaintiff allegedly complied.

The plaintiff further testified that the officer then began to kick both of the plaintiff's feet further apart. As the plaintiff turned his head to tell the officer that he was losing his balance, the officer allegedly, unlawfully and maliciously assaulted and battered him by striking him full on the mouth with a large heavy flashlight.

The plaintiff also alleges that the blow irreparably damaged and broke five of his front teeth and drove the teeth through his lip causing him severe pain and producing profuse bleeding. The officer then, allegedly, issued the plaintiff a citation for resisting arrest.

In the district court trial, the jury cleared the officer and awarded the plaintiff one dollar ($1.00). The judge disagreed with the jury's award and immediately raised it to $10,000.

TANUVASA v. CITY AND COUNTY OF HONOLULU
ET AL, 626 Pacific Reporter, 2d Series 1175 (1981)

When the alleged incident occurred, David Lam was a police officer for the city of Honolulu. The plaintiff, Onasai Tanuvasa, placed the following action against the officer: Action for assault and battery.

The reported facts of the incident are as follows. On the evening of January 3, 1975 Tanuvasa and six friends were gathered in the Kalihi YMCA parking lot talking. Tanuvasa and one other person were in his car; the other five persons were gathering around it. According to the testimony, the group was discussing a camping trip that was to take place later in the evening. The group was being observed by two Honolulu police officers who were watching them through a chainlink fence. The officers were present after they heard what they thought were gunshots in the area. The officers did not see the group conduct any illegal activity.

Officer Lam and another officer approached the group. According to testimony by witnesses, Officer Lam exited his car with a drawn gun in one hand and a flashlight in the other hand. He then ordered the seven up against a nearby wall. Officer Lam denies having a drawn gun.

According to Officer Lam, Tanuvasa was slow to obey his order and asked what was going on. Officer Lam further testified that as Tanuvasa was moving away from the wall, he turned around and pushed Lam with enough force to cause Lam to take a step backward. Tanuvasa was then beat about the head and face with a two-foot long, extremely heavy metal flashlight, by Lam, in what witnesses described as a full-arm swing. Photographs which were introduced as evidence showed that Tanuvasa had one laceration on the face, two on his head, widely separated one from another, which indicates that Lam struck him more than once.

On cross-examination, and after seeing the photographs, Lam admitted to striking Tanuvasa more than once.

Tanuvasa, and the other witnesses, denied that Tanuvasa ever touched Lam or offered any resistance, except to raise his hand to block the blows.

The jury in the lower court returned a verdict against the City and County for general damages in the amount of $250,000, and against Officer Lam for punitive damages in the amount of $6,000. On appeal, the court affirmed the judgement as to Lam and as to the liability of the City and County of Honolulu. The court reversed and remanded for a new trial against the City and County of Honolulu on the issue of general damages only.

UNITED STATES v. GOLDEN, 671 F. 2d 369 (1982)

When the alleged incident occurred, Bobby Ray Golden was a police officer in Nowata, Oklahoma. The plaintiff, United States of America, placed the following action against the officer: Action for violating 18 U.S.C. $ 242, which makes criminal the willful deprivation of constitutional rights by any person acting under color of the law.

The reported facts of the incident are as follows. Officer Golden stopped a motorist for allegedly running a red light at 2:00 a.m. During a discussion with the motorist, Golden hit the motorist on the back of the head with a seven-cell Kel-light flashlight.

After the altercation, the motorist entered his truck and drove 12 miles to his grandmother's house. The evidence shows that enroute to the grandmother's house, the motorist drove at speeds of approximately 120 miles per hour. Upon his arrival, he told his grandmother what had happened, and said that he was fearful for his life.

An FBI agent testified that Golden told him during an interview that he did have a seven-cell Kel-light flashlight with him when he approached the victim's truck. Also during the trial, a defense witness testified that Golden "thumped" the victim with a flashlight on the back of the head. The prosecutor, in an effort to determine what the witness meant, struck a chair back with the flashlight.

The lower court found Golden guilty and sentenced him to serve one year in prison, with all but sixty days suspended, and five years probation. On appeal the Tenth Circuit Court of Appeals affirmed the decision of the lower court.

OTHER CASES

The cases which you have just finished reading are a representative sample of incidents where people were struck by police officers using flashlights. Many other cases exist, too. For example, in **Melina v. Chaplin** (Minnesota, 1981), the court awarded $2,000 in actual damages and $35,000 in punitive damages to the plaintiff. Recently, one California city agreed to pay a flashlight victim $300,000 while another nearby city was ordered to pay $1.25 million dollars to another victim.

Reflecting upon the sentences given to officers and the awards given to the plaintiffs, one must wonder how many of these unfortunate incidents might have been avoided had the officer been provided defensive flashlight or other defensive tactics training. Few will argue that $1.25 million dollars would provide a lot of defensive training for police officers. As we have read, flashlights don't hit people, people who are holding flashlights sometimes do.

Chapter XX

CONCLUSION

The 1980's have already shown an increase in both civil and vicarious liability law suits. And, as clients' attorneys become more skilled in the handling of alleged excessive use of force cases, the trend in such litigation will, no doubt, increase.

The unfortunate aspect of many of these suits is that municipalities, administrators and others are being sued for improperly training their employees, or worse yet, for the failure to train them at all. In **Roberts v. Williams**, 302 F. Supp. 972 (1969) the court ruled that municipalities and police chiefs have a duty to train the officers whom they employ. Hence, the days of handing a police officer a gun (or a flashlight) and a badge, pointing to a police car and then telling him/her to go to work are gone. Training should, and must, take place prior to sending these police officers out to fight crime. If it doesn't, there can only be an increase in this type of litigation.

In an effort to stop this needless litigation, department heads and officers must make a joint commitment to support and then undergo continuous, realistic and professional training. Since continuous training can be costly, it must be viewed like an insurance premium. The money spent by an agency today for training may save it a million dollars tomorrow. With the high damages being awarded in law suits, an agency cannot afford to risk not properly training its personnel.

Unfortunately, many administrators, finance committees, city councils and, yes even officers, only consider training as a **reactive** measure. That is, it is not until an officer or a citizen is killed or seriously injured, or a large court settlement is ordered for the lack of training that a training program is designed and then implemented.

Let's make a commitment to turn the trend of the 1980's around and make it a **proactive** decade, not a **reactive** one. And, when this philosophy is applied to the flashlight, its somewhat tarnished image will again shine bright.

FOOTNOTES

Chapter I
Exhibit I-1:
 Simmons Hardward Company. **Simmons 1918 Complete Catalog.** (Kansas City Lechtman Printing Co., 1917), pp. 773-775.

Exhibit I-2:
 Used with permission, Mag Instrument, Inc.

Chapter II
 [1]Massad Ayoob, "Flashlights and Sidearms: The Latest Techniques... Part I," **Police Marksman,** November-December 1981, p. 10.

Chapter XVI
 [1]Ronald J. Adams, Thomas M. McTernan and Charles Remsberg, **Street Survival Tactics for Armed Encounters** (Illinois: Calibre Press, Inc., 1980), p.49.

Chapter XVIII
John G. Peters, Jr. and Takayuki Kubota, **Realistic Defensive Tactics** (Massachusetts: Defensive Tactics Institute, Inc., 1981), pp. 102-104.

Chapter XIX
Exhibit 19-1:
 Juste David Myers, **Close Quarter Combat,** unpublished manuscript, 1982.

BIBLIOGRAPHY

BOOKS

Adams, Ronald J.; McTernan, Thomas M.; and Remsberg, Charles. **Street Survival Tactics for Armed Encounters.** Illinois: Calibre Press, Inc., 1980.

Ayoob, Massad. **Fundamentals of Modern Police Impact Weapons.** Illinois: Charles C. Thomas, 1978.

_____. **In The Gravest Extreme.** Concord: Wenday Printing, Inc., 1980.

Keller, Donald A. **Kel-Lite Manual of Defensive Tactics.** California: Kel-Lite, _____.

Kubota, Takayuki, and Peters, Jr., John G. **Official Kubotan® Techniques.** Massachusetts: Defensive Tactics Institute, Inc., 1981.

Marshall, Paul W.; Abernathy, William J.; Miller, Jeffrey G.; Olsen, Richard P.; Rosenbloom, Richard S.; and Wycoff, D. Daryl. **Operations Management: Text and Cases.** Illinois: Richard D. Irwin, Inc., 1976.

Mills, Richard L. **Statistics for Applied Economics and Business.** New York: McGraw-Hill Book Company, 1977.

Peters, Jr., John G., and Kubota, Takayuki. **Realistic Defensive Tactics.** Massachusetts: Defensive Tactics Institute, Inc., 1981.

MAGAZINES

Ayoob, Massad. "Selecting the Police Flashlight." **Police Marksman,** March-April 1982, pp. 15-55.

Ayoob, Massad. "Cops and Flashlights." **Police Marksman,** January-February 1982, pp. 18-21.

Ayoob, Massad. "Flashlights and Sidearms: The Latest Techniques... Part I." **Police Marksman,** November-December 1981, pp. 10-15.

Ayoob, Massad. "Dueling Flashlights." **Police Products News,** November 1980, pp. 40-77.

Fallon, Denny. "The Great Flashlight Controversy." **Police Products News,** March 1981, p. 18.

Federal Bureau of Investigation. **The Firing Line** Volume 1, Issue 2, November 1981, p. 3.

INTERVIEWS

Bernstein, Arnold. Albuquerque Police Department. Albuquerque, New Mexico. Interview, July 1982.

Anderson, Dennis. Calibre Press, Inc. Northbrook, Illinois. Interview. August 1982.

Berringer, Howard. Americans For Effective Law Enforcement, San Francisco, California. Interview. August 1982.

Keller, Donald. Mag Instrument. Ontario, California. Interview. August 1982.

Johnson, Ralph. Mag Instrument. Ontario, California. Interview, 3 September 1982.

Fallon, Denny. National Media Group. San Diego, California. Interview. 3 September 1982.

Carley, James. Carley Lamps, Inc. Interview. Torrance, California. Interview, 15 November 1982.